PUBLISHED BY STERLING & ROSS PUBLISHERS
NEW YORK   TORONTO
WWW.STERLINGANDROSS.COM

COVER CHARMAINE O'SAERANG

INTERIOR SARAH HEATH

DESIGN GERI PAPIERNICK

ISBN: 0-9766372-3-5

10 9 8 7 6 5 4 3 2

THE OFFICIAL
CELEBRITY
HANDBOOK

BY

BETH EFRAN & ERIN HINER-GEE

Look Paris, a book for us!

WWW.OFFICIALCELEBRITYHANDBOOK.COM

TABLE OF CONTENTS

INTRODUCTION

CELEBRITY–IN–TRAINING

"Before everything else, getting ready is the secret of success."

Henry Ford -- American Automaker, 1863-1947

So you've decided that you want to become famous. You're sick and tired of seeing everyone else on TV, walking down the red carpet, surrounded by entourages, making lots of money and living a better life than you. If you believe that being successful means being a celebrity then you've come to the right place. As of right now, consider yourself a celebrity-in-training.

Talent helps, but don't think for a minute that's all you'll need. It will take research, determination, planning, and above all, shamelessness. When it comes to achieving fame and keeping it, you'll see that almost nothing is too outrageous. Darva Conger, the reality TV bride who wanted to marry a millionaire but wound up with an annulment, was able to prolong her fame by posing for *Playboy*.

Even reality TV losers can make money and stay famous. Jerri Manthey, the 'survivor' from the Australian Outback that we-love-to-hate, was reportedly paid $1.5 million to pose nude. Jenna Morasca and Heidi Strobel from "Survivor: The Amazon," followed the *Playboy* trend. Even "Joe Millionaire" reject, Sarah Kozer, who has starred in bondage-fetish flicks, has joined the *Playboy* pin-up pack. No guts, no glory.

"The Apprentice" outcasts Kristi Frank, Katrina Campins, Amy Henry and Ereka Vetrini supposedly turned down $250,000 to pose for *Playboy*. Instead, they posed in their underwear for free in *FHM* magazine. No wonder The Donald fired them!

Colby Donaldson, another reality TV runner-up, is the spokesman for Schick Quattro razors, and has guest-starred on "Reba," "Just Shoot Me" and "Curb Your Enthusiasm." Not bad for an auto designer from Christoval, Texas.

Elisabeth Filarski Hasselbeck from Providence, Rhode Island, another reality TV alumnae whose career has 'survived,' is making the most of her time in the limelight in a different way. This shoe designer won the coveted empty seat on ABC's daytime talk show "The View," and has her own show on the Style Network, "The Look For Less."

William "She Bangs" Hung became known for the worst "American Idol" audition ever. Even so, this singing oddity has performed on "The Tonight Show with Jay Leno" and was signed by Koch Records. His 15-song debut album, *Inspiration*, came out in April 2004 and his Christmas album, *Hung for the Holidays*, was a huge success. We told you, you don't exactly need talent to become famous. That's certainly true for the Internet cult figures, the so-called 'Star Wars Kid' and the Numa Numa guy. Now there's 'podcasting,' the Internet version of reality-TV, so it's even easier to embarrass your way to fame.

 Steve Irwin was working at the Australia Zoo when the idea for his television show was hatched. His friend, a television producer, put him on camera and the "The Crocodile Hunter" was born. To date, over 50 episodes of the "Croc Files" have been filmed. His first feature film The Crocodile Hunter - Collision Course was released in 2002. He became even more of a household name when he held his infant son just inches from a crocodile! When he's not competing for the title "Father of the Year," he is working on an animated series and other projects.

Monica Lewinsky, the politically incorrect White House intern, turned her sexual indiscretions into a line of handbags, a tell-all book and a spokeswoman contract with Jenny Craig. She then added TV star to her eclectic bio. After all, who was more qualified to host the dating program "Mr. Personality," than Monica?

Shoshanna Lonstein's claim to fame was that she once dated Jerry Seinfeld. But she used her curvaceous figure and gutsy ambition to develop a line of clothing for the busty. She has also been a style TV reporter and a contributing editor to *Cosmopolitan* magazine.

George Foreman won a medal in the 1968 Olympics, but he's made much more gold since then. He's a boxing commentator for HBO, the pitchman for the *George Foreman Lean Mean Grilling Machine* (over 50 million sold), and the

Comfort Zone clothing line for Casual Male Big & Tall -- deals that have earned him over $100 million.

If they can marry a stranger, survive a diet of rice and backstabbing, make their day jobs paydirt, or turn their misfortune into fortune, then so can you. You don't have to live in a big city or spend a lot of money to become a celebrity, but you do have to be commited. Getting your 15 minutes of fame and then keeping it must be your number one goal. You have to want it ...bad. Your fame defines who you are. You can't breathe or live without it. Every single day, every waking hour, for the rest of your life, you have to chip away at your anonymity. You'll need to jump through hoops, create a buzz, and prove that you're attention ravenous. You can never be too self-involved or media hungry. You've got to use your brains, brawn and yes, sometimes boobs (or the male equivalent.)

In the sixties, Andy Warhol said, "In the future everyone will be famous for 15 minutes." We'll show you how to get your 15 minutes and handle it well, or milk it for a lifetime without becoming a celebrity-in-crisis. And if all else fails, you'll at least learn to feel like the celebrity you were meant to be.

So put your minds at ease, all you fame seekers. Sit back, have your publicist get you a Diet Coke with *crushed ice*, have your manager take off your Jimmy Choos, and we'll get you started.

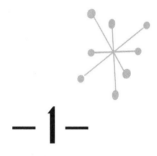

–1–

GETTING THERE

"I want to be famous everywhere."

Luciano Pavarotti -- Italian Tenor

If you're already a hot new celebrity you can skip this chapter. But if you're still hoping to become famous, we'll help you get there. Keep in mind that whether you live in Hollywood or Hoboken, you'll probably have to start at the bottom and claw your way to the top.

Finding Your Niche

First we suggest that you find a niche that will catapult you to stardom. How about broadcasting? Tom Brokaw began his distinguished career at the local Omaha, Nebraska, station KMTV. Katie Couric was a desk assistant at ABC News, and an assignment editor at CNN.

David Letterman got his start at WLWI-TV, an Indianapolis station, as an announcer and weatherman, and had a radio talk show at WNTS before he became famous for his late-night comedy.

Maybe the academic road to fame is for you. Dr. Phillip McGraw from Oklahoma used his brain to become better known as Dr. Phil. He earned a doctorate in psychology, opened a practice and then co-founded Courtroom Sciences, Inc. to help lawyers with mock trials and jury selections. He met Oprah Winfrey when she was being sued by cattlemen and he's been on TV ever since.

Over 20 years ago, Dr. Laura Schlessinger earned a few degrees and became a licensed marriage and family counselor. At the same time, she started working in radio and is now the host of a top-rated talk show.

Judy Sheindlin was prosecuting cases for the state of New York in 1972 where she gained a reputation for being tough and outspoken. She was the subject of a *Los Angeles Times* article in 1993 and was profiled on "60 Minutes." The national exposure led to her Emmy-nominated show "Judge Judy." No one can argue with that.

And of course there are the political bombshells, *blonde* bombshells, that is: Ann Coulter and Laura Ingraham, political conservatives who became famous for hating the Clintons. Ann Coulter wrote *High Crimes and Misdemeanors: The Case Against Bill Clinton,* while Laura Ingraham wrote *The Hillary Trap: Looking for Power in All The Wrong Places.* They used their law degrees, experience in the Senate and White House, clerkship for a Supreme Court Justice, and passion of right-wing politics to propel them into the public arena. Ann Coulter, (*www.anncoulter.com*) makes TV appearances as often as Martha Stewart used to bake cookies, and has scored two *New York Times* best sellers. Laura Ingraham is the host of her own radio show, *(www.lauraingraham.com)* and isn't shy about making TV and newspaper rounds, or wearing a leopard print mini-skirt on the cover of *The New York Times Magazine.*

It's all about finding the venue that's right for you. Does your boss drive you crazy? You could become a famous tattletale. Paul Burrell, Princess Diana's former butler, reportedly made almost $500,000 for selling intimate details of her palace life to London's *Daily Mirror* and wrote the book *A Royal Duty.* Nicola Kraus and Emma McLaughlin wrote the best-selling novel *The Nanny Diaries,* which is believed to be based on some of their real-life experiences as nannies to New York's rich, privileged, and emotionally deprived families. Toby Young didn't cut it at *Vanity Fair,* but he wrote about working with editor-in-chief Graydon Carter and the world of the media elite in his book *How To Lose Friends and Alienate People.* Lauren Weisberger allegedly used her experience working for *Vogue* magazine as the inspiration for her novel *The Devil Wears Prada.*

Would you like to cook your way to fame? Emeril Lagasse, from Fall River, Massachusetts, got a lot of dishes dirty in order to get famous. With a doctorate in culinary arts he worked at countless eateries before he opened his own restaurants to rave reviews. He turned his fame up a notch when he got two cable series and wrote several books. *Bam!*

Julie Powell has found her niche by cooking every dish in Julia Child's book, *Mastering the Art of French Cooking.* This thirty-something secretary began the Julie/Julia Project and along with creating tasty French dishes she developed a web log to record her daily adventures in the kitchen. *The New York Times* wrote a story about her and now she has written stories for them.

Would you rather eat than cook? Ruth Reichl wrote restaurant reviews before she became the restaurant critic for *The New York Times* and wrote two autobiographical bestsellers *Tender at the Bone* and *Comfort Me with Apples*. Now she's the editor-in-chief of *Gourmet* magazine.

Steve "the Bobst Boy" Stanzak got fame and free housing by living in New York University's Bobst Library. He wrote about his housing misfortunes and dedication to education on his website *www.homelessatnyu.com*. *The New York Times*, *New York Newsday*, and *The New York Post* publicized him and the university gave him a free dorm room. Who knows what this adventurous young man will turn his 15 minutes into.

Michael Sheehan has become the "tanning butler" at the Ritz-Carlton in South Beach, Florida. He helps guests apply their tanning products and is applying his newspaper exposure towards a career in modeling.

Or you could become a famous feminist. Gloria Steinem, author and activist, founded *Ms. Magazine*, *(www. msmagazine.com)*, and co-founded several political groups, such as the National Women's Political Caucus, and the Women's Action Alliance. Naomi Wolf wrote the provocative book *The Beauty Myth: How Images of Beauty are Used Against Women* and spurred women everywhere to talk about the cosmetics industry and eating disorders.

Wendy Shanker has gained weight and fame with her new book, *The Fat Girl's Guide to Life*. She's the new expert on chubby chic,*(www.wendyshanker.com)*.

You might find your fame forte as a TV evangelist or a psychic like John Edward, *(www.uni-television.com/johnedward)* and

James Van Praagh, *(www.thebeyondshow.com)*, if dealing with higher powers is more your calling. Monsignor Thomas J. Hartman and Rabbi Marc A. Gellman star as "The God Squad" on their national cable television show. These good friends can also be seen on ABC's "Good Morning America" and heard on "Imus in the Morning," and have written a number of books.

Are you interested in finding celebrities on the lamb? You could become a famous bounty hunter. Duane Lee Chapman,(shown here with his son) nicknamed "Dog," found fame, not to mention convicted rapist and heir to the Max Factor fortune Andrew Luster, in Mexico. This publicity hound, *(www. dogthebountyhunter.com)*, has been on the lecture circuit, and now has his own show on A&E entitled "Dog the Bounty Hunter."

If you'd rather take their picture than put them in jail, become a celebrity photographer. Richard Avedon and Annie Leibovitz have turned their fabulous photos into art and museum exhibits and have made a fortune shutter-bugging.

If you have a good eye and good taste, then decorate your way to fame. Christopher Lowell, *(http://christopherlowell. com)*, spent big bucks filming his lectures and editing them into a pilot. Now he has his own show on The Discovery Channel and writes decorative bestsellers. Colin Cowie threw parties and was a guest on talk shows before he hosted "Everyday Elegance with Colin Cowie" on American Movie Classics, Romance Classics and wrote *Colin Cowie's Weddings* and *Effortless Entertaining with Colin Cowie*. Now he has a show on Women's Entertainment (WE), *(www.*

colincowie.com). Doug Wilson, (http://tlc.discovery.com), is the celebrity decorator of the TV show "Trading Spaces."

Getting Noticed

Now do you see what we mean by niche? Once you've decided on your special niche it's time to cultivate your fame and get noticed. You can intern at your local or college TV and radio stations. The website *www.tvjobs.com* or the job bank at *www.emmyonline.org* list openings at your nearest station. *Broadcasting and Cable* magazine, *(www.broadcastingcable. com)*, has job listings as well.

•MUST DO•

If you're looking at getting in front of the camera immediately you have to get a little more creative. After you've slipped your foot in the door at a TV station, befriend the nicest cameraman so he'll help you make a reel, which is simply a video showcase of what you can do. Use your reel to convince management that you should be on the air, in the capacity that you're interested in (decorator, weatherperson, film critic, news anchor, singer). In the beginning, you may be fetching coffee for all the reporters (with a happy attitude and smile on your face), but your secret, number one goal is to get on TV. (And make sure it stays secret- there's no quicker way to get blacklisted than for your co-workers to find out you're gunning for their job.)

Page or Intern

Or you could start as a TV Page or intern. Regis Philbin, Michael Eisner, Ted Koppel, Willard Scott, Kate Jackson and many other celebrities began as pages. Brian Unger's first job in television was as an intern at CBS' "The Late Show with David Letterman." Later he became a producer and correspondent on the "Daily Show" and then a co-host of "Extra." Now he's on National Public Radio (NPR) and is the host of Fox's "World's Craziest Videos."

Entry-Level Job Resources

www.nbcjobs.com or e-mail the page program, *capage@nbc.com*, for California, and *nypage@nbc.com* for New York opportunities.
www.cbsdiversity.com/internship.shtml or e-mail *cbsjobs@tvc.cbs.com* for Los Angeles, and *CBSpageprogram@cbs.com* for page jobs in New York
http://jobsearch.disneycareers.newjobs.com
http://jobhuntweb.viacom.com
www.wbjobs.com
www.foxcareers.com
www.showbizjobs.com
www.showbizmonster.com

•*DID YOU KNOW?*•

Barry Manilow started his career in the CBS mailroom. He delivered Walter Cronkite's mail before he wrote the songs that made the whole world sing. *(www.barrymanilow.com)*.

Rita Tateel, a celebrity expert, founded The Celebrity Source, Inc., *(www.celebritysource.com)*. She wrangles major Hollywood stars and gets them to appear at special star-studded events.

If you have a strong stomach and a head for business, like Bill Rancic, take a shot at becoming Donald Trump's new apprentice, *(www.nbc.com/The_Apprentice/)*. Or you might become famous for getting fired by him, like everyone's least favorite meddler Omarosa Manigault-Stallworth.

Are you still in school? There are many celebrities who were once cheerleaders. It's a great way to get your first taste of fame and warm to the gaze of the spotlight. According to sources, Paula Abdul, Halle Berry, Calista Flockhart, Cybill Shepherd, Teri Hatcher, Meryl Streep, Sandra Bullock, Katie Couric, and even George W. Bush know a thing or two about pom-poms.

You could create your own website and enter popular chat rooms, (under an assumed name, of course) to promote yourself like crazy. This worked for Emily Gimmel, a young reporter for WKYT-TV in Lexington, Kentucky. The link to her website, *(www.emilygimmel.com)*, ended up in a chat room and created such noise that it caught the eye of a newspaper journalist, who then wrote about her. Her star is definitely on the rise.

Laurel Touby was a contributing editor for *Glamour* magazine, then became an entrepreneur and cyber-hostess. Her website *www.mediabistro.com*, features job and events listings and attracts hundreds of thousands of media professionals. Her online community meets in the real world for seminars and panel discussions, and invitation-only cocktail and dinner parties. Through word of mouth, Touby has become one of the most talked-about media industry organizers in the country. She might just help you get your first job.

Get on public access television. Since the age of 14 Michael Essany has hosted a late- night talk show out of his parents' house in Valparaiso, Indiana. He began by sending out 300 letters to celebrities he wanted to interview. Believe it or not, guests such as Kevin Bacon, Carrot Top, Tom Green, Jewel, and Joey McIntyre actually traveled to his home to be on his show. After six years of broadcasting on public access television, his show was picked up by E! Entertainment

Network, *(www.eonline.com/On/Essany/index.html)*, and can now be seen across the nation. Jay Leno -- watch out!

Ken Kleiber has his own Manhattan cable television show, "That's Kentertainment," *(www.thatskentertainment.com)*. He was the first to get an exclusive interview with Liza Minnelli after her breakup with husband David. The list of celebrities he's interviewed is indeed impressive: Cyndi Lauper, Woody Allen, Alan Cumming, and more. As he states, "Any schmo can have a cable TV show! Just present your paperwork, including proof of New York City residency, at the Manhattan Neighborhood Network, and you're on your way!"

Do you like the sound of your own voice? Do others? If what you crave is recognition and admiration by your peers and co-workers, and you can live without the adulation of the masses, then becoming an announcer or voice-over artist may be just right for you. You could become the voice of commercials, television news programs, movie trailers, telephone menus, and so on. *The Ross Reports* also puts out the *Animation and Voice-Over Casting Directory.*

Wendell Craig, *(http://anncrman.com)*, is an announcer and one of the recognizable voices of CBS News, as well as many other gigs (commercials, promos, and radio and TV show introductions). He says there are several common ways to get started in this "almost famous" business, "the two most common being through broadcasting or theater. You can hone your chops at a local radio or TV station, or by joining a local theater group, which is the route chosen by many of my friends. And these days with the advent of ISDN (Integrated Services Digital Network) and other instant communications technologies, you don't even need to live in one of the three or four biggest cities to make a respectable living."

According to Craig, "If you're good, and work real hard, and get some breaks along the way, the pay ain't all that bad, too! Ranging from a low of zero dollars a year, to a reported six million!"

Want to become a famous sports announcer like Howard Cosell? The S.I. Newhouse School of Public Communications, (*http://newhouse.syr.edu/*), has a great reputation if you want a career in broadcasting or journalism. Also check out www.journalismjobs.com. Is it your "Dream Job" to be ESPN's SportsCenter anchor? Go to *http://espn.illiad.com* to find out how to compete to get your one-year contract.

•DID YOU KNOW?•

World-renowned sports announcer and entertainer Michael Buffer, (*www.letsrumble.com*), made a career out of the trademark phrase, "Let's get ready to rumble." Wholesale licensing revenues have grossed an estimated $150 million over the past few years.

On the Write Track

Write, write, and write. Write letters and send them to David Letterman's mailbag, (*www.cbs.com/latenight/lateshow/show_info/#*), and maybe he'll answer them on his show, or write to the editors of newspapers just to get your name in print. Write for your school or town newspaper. Make sure you find a beat that everyone in your community is talking about. If basketball is the hot topic then become the team reporter. Who knows, you may be covering the next $90 million Nike-wearing/basketball playing LeBron James.

Helen Gurley Brown came from the sticks of Arkansas, but became a publishing phenomenon. This editor-extraordinaire of *Cosmopolitan* started as a secretary and an advertising copywriter before writing the bestseller, *Sex and the Single Girl*, several other books and a newspaper column, starting a magazine, and marrying successful movie and Broadway producer David Brown. She was definitely the Carrie Bradshaw of her generation.

Write that novel or short story you always wanted to and then use reference books like *Literary Agents* by Debby Mayer or websites like *www.publishersmarketplace.com* and *www. literarymarketplace.com* to help get your work published. Stephen King worked in a laundry factory and had stories rejected by *Spacemen* magazine, *Alfred Hitchcock's Mystery Magazine, Fantasy and Science Fiction* magazine, and *Ellery Queen's Mystery Magazine*, before he made his first real money with the novel *Carrie*.

In the King's Foot Steps
Alfred Hitchcock's Mystery Magazine
www.themysteryplace.com
Ellery Queen's Mystery Magazine
www.themysteryplace.com
Red Herring Mystery Magazine
e-mail *rhmmag@aol.com*

G.P. Taylor, a British vicar, is the author of *Shadowmancer, (www.shadowmancer.com)*, which spent 15 weeks on the bestsellers list in the United Kingdom. He wrote the manuscript in only nine months, and then sold his motorcycle for the money to have it self-published. Now he's about to make millions in movie rights and multi-book deals. Are you inspired yet?

Writer's Relief, *www.writersrelief.com*, is an author's submission service. Write that short story and they'll peddle it for you by looking through literary journals and magazines to find a venue for your work. You write it and they promote it, once it's submitted and accepted. Good luck.

Write that screenplay you always wanted to. Robert McKee gives screenwriting seminars, (*http://mckeestory.com*), so you can learn to write screenplays like a pro. You can also check out screenwriting programs, such as Final Draft, (*www.finaldraft.com*), and books on how to write film and TV treatments at *www.writersstore.com*. Once you're done, register your screenplay with the Writers Guild of America, (*www.wga.org*). Or you could always start your writing career by reading other people's scripts and earn money working on 'coverage reports.'

COVERAGE REPORT EXAMPLE

Your Name:

OVERALL: (you will either PASS or ACCEPT for review)

TITLE: Fashion Cops   **SUBMITTED TO:**
AUTHOR: **SUBMITTED BY:**

                                   SUBMISSION DATE:

TYPE OF MATERIAL: Screenplay/number of pages

GENRE: COMEDY/DRAMA   **CIRCA:** The Present

SETTING: Manhattan

ELEMENTS

PREMISE: Fair   **CHARACTERS:** Fair

DIALOGUE: Good   **PLOT:** Non-existent

	EXCELLENT	GOOD	FAIR	POOR
PREMISE			X	
DIALOGUE		X		
CHARACTERS			X	
PLOT				X

LOGLINE: Joe, an East Village fashion cop, acquires something other than a new outfit -- the love of his life.

(A logline is a snazzy one-sentence description of the screenplay.)

BRIEF COMMENTS: This script is reminiscent of *RoboCop* and *Clueless*, but lacks one important thing -- a plot in which the characters actually have a chance to develop, and the reader actually has a chance to care about them.

SYNOPSIS: Summarize the plot here.

COMMENTS: The characters are very clear. They are very superficial and that is exactly what they are supposed to be. The dialogue suits the characters, and their voices are strong.

The consistency is refreshing, but the characters are one-dimensional. Since there is not much of a plot, this script is character-driven, but the characters are not interesting enough to sustain a whole film. When Joe's life turns out fabulously at the end, the reader wonders why good things happen to stupid people.

•*DID YOU KNOW?*•

If you think you don't have the time to write -- think again. John Hughes reportedly wrote "The Breakfast Club" in 48 hours, and Sylvester Stallone wrote "Rocky" and Stephen King wrote *The Running Man* in just one week. The screenplay for the movie *Open Water* was written in approximately six days.

Fox has a creative writer development department geared towards finding, supporting and showcasing the next great television writers, (*www.fox.com/creativewriter*). Or hook up with a buddy and write a screenplay together. Friends Matt Damon and Ben Affleck wrote the Academy Award winning screenplay, *Good Will Hunting*.

Actor Kevin Spacey formed Trigger Street Productions, Inc. in 1997. Now there's *www.triggerstreet.com*, a website devoted to showcasing and discovering filmmakers and screenwriters. Can you work up the nerve to have others read your screenplay? Posting it on the website might just get some positive critiques and a foot in the door.

Direct Approach

You could apply for the Directors Guild of America Training Program and get on-the-job assistant director movie experience and maybe become a famous director like Steven Spielberg and Martin Scorsese. Luckily, you don't have to be a union member to apply. At *www.trainingplan.org* you'll find the information for the West Coast, and *www.dgatrainingprogram.org* for the East Coast. Project Greenlight, the Matt Damon/Ben Affleck venture, always has contests to enter, (*http://projectgreenlight.liveplanet.com*).

You can also apply to film school. Some of these schools even have summer programs and workshops if you're not ready to commit to being a full-time film student.

Film Schools
American Film Institute
www.afi.com
University of California at Los Angeles
www.tft.ucla.edu
University of Southern California
www-cntv.usc.edu
New York University Film School
www.tisch.nyu.edu/page/home
Columbia University School of the Arts
www.columbia.edu/cu/arts/film

•DID YOU KNOW?•
Martin Scorsese went to NYU's Film School
in the 1960's.

•MUST DO•
If you're going to be hanging around Hollywood movie sets, you have to know how to break down scripts. Everyone will be talking about this at meetings, so you'll definitely want to understand what this means. Every once in a while the DGA offers seminars on this skill, so check out *www.dga.org*. And the screenwriting program Final Draft 7, (*www.finaldraft.com*), has just come out with a new feature designed to help transfer script information to breakdown sheets.

Breaking down a script involves analyzing all the different categories and then figuring out what elements you will need for each scene. It's the associate director's job to make sure everything is ready for the director to shoot. By using highlighters, you'll color-code each category such as cast, props, wardrobe, animals, music, and vehicles. Each speaking role, or cast member, gets an assigned number that every department will use. The highlighted information for each scene gets transferred to a breakdown sheet, which is eventually used for all schedules, reports and budgets. If this seems complicated and important, that's because it is! In fact, breaking down a script can be incredibly complex, but it's also imperative that you know how to do this. Make sure you learn to do it the right way.

Animal Attraction

If you're "Nuts for Mutts," *www.nutsformutts.com*, maybe Fido has what it takes to get you some TV time. The Animal Planet network is looking for funny animals and pets with problems. Make a tape and send it. (*www.animal.discovery. com/features/getonshow/getonshow.html*)

Planet's Funniest Animals
P.O. Box 2904
Toluca Lake, CA 91610-0904
E-mail *animalplanet@painless.tv*

Pet Star
P.O. Box 2900
Toluca Lake, CA 91610
323-463-5040
If you always wanted to work at the zoo, you might be ready to take the crocodile challenge. Ten contestants will be selected to work at the Australia Zoo alongside the Crocodile Hunter, (*http://animal.discovery.com*)_.

One of the quickest ways to get your 15 minutes of fame is

to become an audience member or guest on a talk show.

Talk Shows
Jenny Jones
www.jennyjones.com
Maury Povich
www.uni-television.com/maury
Jerry Springer
www.jerryspringer.com
Montel Williams
www.montelshow.com

Even if you're not a celebrity yet, this doesn't mean you can't get some airtime on the higher-end talk shows, especially if your story's interesting enough. You can e-mail your story ideas to Oprah, at *www.oprah.com/email/email_landing. jhtml*. You could also be a guest on the Ellen DeGeneres Show, *http://ellen.warnerbros.com/showinfo/guests/index. html*.

•DID YOU KNOW?•
Mindy Burbano was in the audience of "The Oprah Winfrey Show" and it radically changed her life. She was a dental hygienist from Michigan who happened to have a funny talent -- she can crow like rooster. A local TV station spotted this so-called "rooster lady," and she landed a job as a reporter. Her star was on the rise when she was hired as a reporter for "Entertainment Tonight." In Las Vegas, she met her future husband, who just happened to be a millionaire! She became a reporter for the Los Angeles station KTLA, lives in a multi-million dollar mansion and is driven around by a chauffeur. Keep in mind that all this started because she went to a taping of a television talk show.

Many people have no trouble making their personal problems public by talking to Dr. Phil, (www.drphil.com), or exposing their old junk at "Antiques Roadshow." Go to www.pbs.org to find out when the show is coming to your city.

Game Show Auditions

Go on a game show and win some TV attention and maybe even some moola.

www.seeingstars.net/ShowBiz/index.shtml

www.thelivingweb.net/how_to_be_on_tv.html

"Who Wants to be a Millionaire"
www.millionairetv.com

"Jeopardy!"
www.jeopardy.com

"The Price is Right"
www.cbs.com/daytime/price or call 323-575-2449

"Wheel of Fortune"
www.wheeloffortune.com

"Pyramid"
www.sonypictures.com/tv/shows/pyramid

TV Judges

Feeling litigious? Plead your case to a TV judge.

"Judge Judy"
www.judgejudy.com
"Judge Hatchett"
www.sonypictures.com/tv/shows/judgehatchett/

"Judge Joe Brown"
www.judgejoebrown.com/submitcase/submitcase.asp
Court TV
www.courttv.com/contact/
"Judge Mathis"
www.judgemathis.net/yourcase.htm or
call 1-800-VERDICT
"The People's Court"
http://peoplescourt.warnerbros.com

So You Really Want to be an Actor?

If you've decided that you really want to be an actor then you've got to start somewhere. Brad Pitt wore a chicken suit for El Pollo Loco and worked as a limo driver for strippers in order to pay for acting lessons, until he landed a role on the soap "Another World." Meg Ryan made toothpaste and Burger King commercials, and spent two years on "As The World Turns." Demi Moore was on "General Hospital." Julianne Moore even won an Emmy for playing two-half sisters, Frannie and Sabrina, on "As The World Turns." Sarah Michelle Gellar, Lea Thompson and Elisabeth Shue all appeared in the same Burger King commercial together. Not a bad cast for a burger joint!

Former Soap Opera Actors

Kevin Bacon	"Guiding Light"
Alec Baldwin	"The Doctors"
Ted Danson	"Somerset"
Laurence Fishburne	"One Life to Live"
Morgan Freeman	"Another World"
Sarah Michelle Gellar	"All My Children"

Tommy Lee Jones	"One Life to Live"
Robin Wright Penn	"Santa Barbara"
John Stamos	"General Hospital"
Sigourney Weaver	"Somerset"
JoBeth Williams	"Somerset"

Daytime Casting

Send your headshot and résumé only. Most soaps won't take your phone call or screen your videotapes, so don't even try.

New York
"All My Children" -- *http://abc.go.com/site/faq.html#10*
320 W. 66th Street, NY, NY 10023

"As The World Turns" -- *www.cbs.com/daytime*
1268 E.14th Street, Brooklyn, NY 11230

"Guiding Light" -- *www.cbs.com/daytime*
CBS, 51 W. 52nd Street, New York, NY 10019 and 222 E. 44th Street, NY, NY 10017

"One Life To Live" -- *http://abc.go.com/site/faq.html#10*
157 Columbus Avenue, 2nd Floor, NY, NY 10023

Los Angeles
"The Bold and the Beautiful" -- *www.cbs.com/daytime*
Bell-Phillip Television, 7800 Beverly Blvd., Suite 3371,
Los Angeles, CA 90036

"Days of Our Lives" -- *www.nbc.com*
3000 West Alameda Avenue, Burbank, CA 91523

"General Hospital"/"Port Charles" -- *http://abc.go.com/site/*

faq.html#10 4151 Prospect Avenue, Studio 54, 5th Floor, Los Angeles, CA 90027

"Passions" -- *www.nbc.com/nbc/Passions/youasked2.shtml* 4024 Radford Avenue, Studio City, CA 91604

"The Young and The Restless" -- *www.cbs.com/daytime* Bell-Phillip Television, 7800 Beverly Blvd., Suite 3305, Los Angeles, CA 90036

If your friends and family still haven't talked you out of it, keep in mind that the competition between actors, singers, and entertainers is fierce, so you have to be resourceful. You can never do too much or go too far, as long as it's legal. Use your contacts and network. For better or for worse, nepotism makes the world go around. You could call your friend's cousin's brother's uncle who's a film crew caterer and ask him to get you a job as a production assistant or score you some auditions.

•MUST HAVE•

If you're trying to get your foot in the door as a production assistant, you must have at least two kinds of stopwatches, digital and analog, different colored pens, highlighters, a clipboard, and baked goods or candy to motivate (read: bribe) the crew to do what you want them to.

ON STAGE

Perform, perform, and perform. Nia Vardalos reportedly wrote the first draft of the one-woman play "My Big Fat Greek Wedding" in two weeks and then performed it. The play was a hit and got the attention of Rita Wilson and Tom Hanks who helped turn it onto an Academy Award nominated movie.

Find the open-mike night at a comedy club. *Ha!* is a comedy club in New York City that hosts open-mike nights once a week and fills approximately 200 spots a week with "Seinfeld" wannabes, *(www.hacomedynyc.com)*. Mike Bullard hosts an open-mike show in Canada on the Comedy Network, *(www.thecomedynetwork.ca)*, if you're heading up north. The Ross Reports has a Comedy Casting Guide that lists comedy clubs across the nation. And keep checking the NBC network, *(www.nbc.com)*, because you never know when Jay Mohr's "Last Comic Standing" will return for another season. It's also a good idea to check out the New York Comedy Festival, *www.newyorkcomedyfestival.com*.

•DID YOU KNOW?•

British comedian sensation and satirist Sacha Baron Cohen worked in restaurants and comedy clubs before he had his own show called "Da Ali G Show" on HBO, *(www.hbo.com/alig)*.

If you're between the ages of 8-18 you might take your first steps towards fame at the Stage Door Manor Performing Arts Training Center, *(www.stagedoormanor.com)*. It's a total theater immersion summer camp. Alums include Natalie Portman, Jon Cryer, Mandy Moore and Robert Downey, Jr. You can also apply for a job there at *info@stagedoorjobs.com*.

•DID YOU KNOW?•

Jennifer Aniston is one of the notable alums that attended the Fiorello H. LaGuardia High School of Music & Art and Performing Arts, *(www.laguardiahs.org)*, the school that the movie and TV show "Fame" is based on.

Some Famous LaGuardia High School Alums

Ellen Barkin	James Burrows
Steven Bochco	Liza Minelli
Adrien Brody	Al Pacino
Wesley Snipes	Suzanne Vega
Sarah Michelle Gellar	

Modeling

Maybe you could get your feet wet in the modeling biz by working at boat and car shows. Check out these websites to find out when a show is coming to a city near you.

Discover Boating Boat Show Tour
www.boatshows.com
United States Boat Shows
www.usboat.com
Car Show News and Classic Auto Events
www.carshownews.com
Car Shows
www.car-shows.com

See what's going on at your local mall. During prom season stores like JC Penney and Sears host dress extravaganzas, so become one of their models. Some of the higher-end modeling agencies send scouts on the lookout for supermodels. The Elite Model Look Event kicked off its 2004 season at the Eastwood Mall in Ohio. Girls walked down runways in front of Elite scouts. You could also send a videotape of yourself to your UPN affiliate to enter Tyra Banks' show, "America's Next Top Model." The website *www.upn.com* will lead you to the address and contact information of your nearest station.

•DID YOU KNOW?•

Tiffany, the 80's pop star, became famous for gathering crowds on her musical mall tours. Matt LeBlanc was a Levi's model before he became Joey from "Friends." Supermodel Linda Evangelista entered the 1988 Miss Teen Niagara Contest at the age of 15. Even though she didn't win, entering the contest was just the first step to her climb to the modeling top. A modeling scout discovered her at the contest and her star rose from there. It's hard to believe she didn't win. (In fact, we wonder what happened to the winner.)

Modeling Agencies

Boss Models
www.bossmodels.com
Click Model Management
www.clickmodel.com
Elite Model Management
www.elitemodellookusa.com and
www.elitemodel.com
Ford Models
www.fordmodels.com
IMG Models
www.imgworld.com
New York Models
www.newyorkmodels.com
Next Models
www.nextmodels.com
Q Model Management
www.qmodels.com
Storm Models
www.stormmodels.com
Wilhelmina Models
www.wilhelmina.com

The website *www.newfaces.com* has lists of top modeling agencies. *www.mymodelingagency.com* has links to *www. models.com*, *www.modelscouts.com*, and other modeling websites. *www.supermodel.com* lists modeling services, agencies, and model search contests. At *www.supermodels-online.com* you can read all about supermodels and find links to some of the top modeling agencies and open calls.

Why not enter your local beauty contest? You can find all the state pageant information at *www.pageantclub. com* and subscribe to *Pageantry Magazine* at *www. pageantrymagazine.com* for tips on how to get the winning look.

•*DID YOU KNOW?*•

Deborah Norville, *www.dnorville.com*, was Junior Miss Georgia in 1976, and Diane Sawyer, *http:// abcnews.go.com*, was Junior Miss America in 1963.

Auditions and Casting Calls

Audition for commercials or soap operas or for anything! It's now your full-time job to research casting agents and then mail them your photo and résumé. *The Ross Reports* is the most complete guide for finding casting agents and directors for television and film. The booklet also lists movies that are in development and in preparation and production companies. No self-respecting celebrity wannabe should be without this guide. For casting contacts across the country *The Ross Reports* publishes the *USA Talent Directory: A Nationwide Guide to Agents & Casting Directors*. *The Ross Reports* also produces *The Film Casting & Production Directory*, which includes movie studio executives, a section on film festivals, production companies, and talent agents. You can get online subscriptions at *www.backstage.com*.

Thank your lucky stars or Al Gore that the Internet was invented. It's an actor's/performer's best friend. Now with the tips of your fingers you can search like crazy for casting calls in your hometown or a town near you. Here are some examples:

Back Stage online, very reputable
www.backstage.com/backstage/casting/index.jsp
Source for free audition information
www.actornews.com
Casting services for NYC
www.actorsreps.com
Resource for auditions and casting calls
www.auditions.net
"The industry's online directory"
www.showbiz.com
Talent directory, but you need to register
www.castingyou.com

•MUST DO•

Once you get a credit for a film, commercial or anything of that genre, make sure you get it listed on The Internet Movie Database at www.imdb.com -- this is what all the production houses use too!

•DID YOU KNOW?•

Since it's the 21st century, you can now post or submit your headshot and résumé electronically. You can check out www.myeshots.com and www.backstage.com for examples. Website www.talentmatch.com says it's "the world's #1 indie community." Whether you're an actor, director, DJ, model, dancer, musician, comedian, artist or writer, or any combination of the above, you can post your entire portfolio online at this site, and get feedback, press, showcases, and hopefully even movie roles.

•MUST HAVE•

You must have a professional headshot and résumé. Andrew Eccles and Nigel Barker have shot some of the contestants on "America's Next Top Model." Kevin Mazur, Mario Testino, Bruce Weber, Tiziano Magni, Arthur Elgort, Greg Gorman, John Falocco, and David Hiller are other big names in the photography game, but if you can't afford to book them you should look for local photographers with good reputations and experience. The website *www.stagesource.org* can give you some headshot and résumé guidance. We recommend that you be yourself, look your age, and use black and white photography. It's the only acceptable form in Hollywood. Some places will accept electronic headshots, others won't. Don't try to fight it. When it comes to headshots, give them what they want or they won't want you.

(By the same token, if you happen to fall into some bad luck and get arrested, for shoplifting or lewd behavior, for example, don't let your hideous mug shot ruin your career. Run a comb through your hair before they take that photo and go easy on the lipstick, especially if you're supposed to be a guy!)

The Hollywood Reporter, www.hollywoodreporter.com, has production charts and *Back Stage* has hundreds of casting notices for theater, film and television. Use your fingertips, *we can't say that often enough!* The Internet has websites, such as *www.entertainmentcareers.net*, that lists movie and local TV casting calls.

•*DID YOU KNOW?*•

Even your local government might help you find fame. For example, at the New York City government website, *www.nyc.gov/html/film/html/home/reeljobs.shtml*, you can search for jobs in the performing arts. You might just have to thank your mayor during your award acceptance speech.

Reality TV

Let's face it -- MTV's "The Real World" was the grandmother of all the other reality TV shows that exist today. It's now in its 15th season! You can check out audition information by going to the MTV website, *www.mtv.com*, and searching under "The Real World."

•*DID YOU KNOW?*•

Kelley Limp, a former cast member on 2000's "The Real World: New Orleans" married "Party of Five" actor Scott Wolf. Now that's going from the real world to a dream world!

You can search the Internet for the newest reality TV show casting calls, audition announcements, news, and links to your favorite programs. Keep visiting these websites because new reality TV shows are popping up all over the place, especially during the summer, when regular programming goes into reruns. Fox is even starting an all-reality all-the-time TV cable channel, so your reality TV fame can keep going. Some reality shows die quietly by the wayside, so don't let this surprise you, or else they'll suddenly get resurrected without notice.

News and reality TV information
www.realitytvworld.com
Casting call notices and links to the official TV show websites
www.realitytvlinks.com
News and casting calls
www.orwellproject.com
News, schedules, and casting information
www.realitytvcalendar.com

If it's your dream to be a reality TV star, you might not want to waste precious competitive application time. You can cut to the chase and search the network websites directly to find reality TV casting calls and online applications for each program. Don't be timid! Search like crazy and you'll find what's being planned and what new shows are being created. This year ABC came up with its own version of "The Apprentice" called "The Benefactor." The WB is looking for college-aged contestants to live together and compete on a quiz show. Ever wondered if you had what it takes to follow in entrepreneur extraordinaire Richard Branson's footsteps? Maybe you could be a contestant on his new reality TV show on Fox, "The Rebel Billionaire: Branson's Quest for the Best."

Casting notices for ABC reality TV
http://abc.go.com/site/casting.html
Here you can find casting calls for the WB affiliates
www.thewb.com
"The Rebel Billionaire: Branson's Quest for the Best"
www.fox.com
Become a contestants on an NBC show
www.nbc.com/nbc/footer/Contestants.shtml
VH1 reality TV casting calls
www.vh1.com/shows/casting_call

MTV reality TV casting calls
www.mtv.com/onair/castingcall
"Big Brother" online application
www.cbs.com/primetime/bigbrother_application
"Amazing Race" application
www.cbs.com/primetime/amazing_race_application
E! Entertainment Television
www.eonline.com/On/Shows/Signup
"Queer Eye for the Straight Guy" questionnaire
www.thequeereye.com/Be_on_the_Show

Do you have what it takes to survive and compete in remote locations without food? Apply to be on "Survivor" at *www.cbs.com/primetime/survivor_application*. Does your relationship have what it takes to survive long-term? Bravo's looking for some brave couples to expose how they really feel about each other at *www.walltowallmedia.com/Show.asp*.

Do you want to become the next Britney Spears, Christina Aguilera, LeAnn Rimes or Alanis Morissette? They were all on "Star Search." Check out *www.cbs.com/primetime/star_search_application* for audition information. Do you want to become the next Kelly Clarkson or Ruben Studdard? Go to *www.idolonfox.com*. Is there a diva inside you? Maybe you're tough enough to take your chances on "Showtime at the Apollo," (*www.apolloshowtime.com*). Do you want to shake your "groove thing" in public? Find out when "Soul Train" is heading to your town, (*www.soultrain.com*).

•DID YOU KNOW?•

Brad Garrett from "Everybody Loves Raymond," (*www.everybodylovesray.com*) was the first $100,000 champion in the 1984 "Star Search" comedy category.

Come up with your own reality TV show idea and pitch

it to the networks. We came up with "The Quitters." Ten three-pack-a-day smokers are picked to live in a house and quit smoking cold turkey: no patch, no nicotine gum. They are given challenges such as running up a flight of stairs, sitting at a bar in difficult social situations, and drinking their morning coffee without lighting up. The winner takes all -- a million bucks.

•*DID YOU KNOW?*•

The Academy of Television Arts and Sciences, (*www. emmys.com*), has created a new category called "Reality/Competition Program." CBS' "The Amazing Race" won in this category two years in a row.

Extra Work

You could become a movie or TV show extra, or even an award show seat-filler. Sylvia Fay Casting and Grant Wilfley Casting hire the extras for the "Law & Order" series. You could wind up serving jury duty on a courtroom drama. Many other television shows, such as "The Practice" and "CSI" get their extras from the Central Casting agency.

Extras Casting

Central Casting
www.entertainmentpartners.com
Grant Wilfley Casting
www.grantwilfleycasting.com
Sylvia Fay Casting
71 Park Avenue, New York, NY 10016

•MUST KNOW•

You must know the names by which the important casting directors are called. For example, brilliant casting director Juliet Taylor's nickname is actually "Muffy" to the people who really know her.

•MUST DO•

Sooner or later you'll want to become a union member. Doing extra or commercial work is a great way to get your union card. Call the Screen Actors Guild at 323-549-6772 or go to *www.sag.org* to find out how to become a member, or if you're already a member go to their website to check out their job hotline.

If you're performing a job that is under AFTRA (American Federation of Television and Radio Artists) jurisdiction, including commercial work, then you're eligible for membership. Go to *www.aftra.org* for more information. If you want to be on Broadway, the website *http://web.actorsequity.org/CastingSearch/* has membership information for theater actors, audition listings, casting calls and photo/résumé requests.

•MUST DO•

After your audition always send a thank-you note. It will show that you're a considerate and thoughtful person. It's also an opportunity to show your creativity. You could send a thank-you note along with your own headshot calendar made on your computer. Check out *www.shutterfly.com*, for examples.

Being Seen

It's critical to be seen over and over again at the right places. We suggest you check out the trendiest restaurants in your town or city and constantly make an appearance. Any nightclub that is just opening may be a way to start. Bartending at a hot spot is a good idea. It will allow you to meet the who's who of your town. Make sure you only go where the local movers and shakers socialize because they're the ones who can help you at this stage. Hosting may be the only gig for you, because in many small towns the wait staff is still snubbed. Being a hostess also carries a bit of clout and allows you room for informal conversation. Is there a country club that <u>everyone</u> belongs to? If you have an idea for a film this may be where you find your funding.

Former Waitresses
Gillian Anderson
Jennifer Aniston
Sandra Bullock
Minnie Driver
Kristin Davis
Rachel Griffiths
Jessica Lange
Debi Mazur
Julianne Moore
Lea Thompson

Former Waiters
Kevin Bacon
Robin Williams

Former Bartenders
Liev Schreiber
Bruce Willis

Former Hostesses
Patricia Heaton
Ashley Judd

•Did You Know?•

Some of Hollywood's superstars made ends meet working at fast-food joints. Bill Murray and Stephen Baldwin worked in pizza parlors. Andie MacDowell worked at Pizza Hut and McDonald's. Madonna worked at Dunkin' Donuts, and Queen Latifah worked at Burger King.

The Name Game

Consider changing your name. Ralph Lauren was born Ralph Lifschitz, but would anyone buy $300 bed sheets from a guy named Lifschitz? Lucille Ball was Dianne Belmont, Whoopi Goldberg was Caryn Johnson, Queen Latifah was born Dana Owens, and Carmen Electra was Tara Patrick. Yusuf Islam was singer Cat Stevens who was Steven Demetre Georgiou, but that's a whole different story. Of course, if you're really famous you can get away with just one name, for example, Cher, Oprah, Madonna, Sting, Jesus, and don't forget Omarosa.

•MUST DO•

Be aware of rule number 15 of the Screen Actors Guild Membership Rules and Regulations:

"It is the Guild's objective that no member use a professional name which is the same as, or resembles so closely as to tend to be confused with, the name of any other member...The Guild urges all applicants and members to minimize any personal or individual risk of liability by avoiding a name that may cause confusion." (*www.sag.org*)

In other words, the names Brad Pitt, Julia Roberts and George Clooney are already taken, so you'll have to be creative and come up with an original name of your own. How about Seymour Johnson, Roxy Bare and Harry Buttons? Michael Keaton's real name was Michael Douglas, but there was already a Michael Douglas, so he changed it.

Once you've gained some confidence, you can take your mingling on the road. Find out about the film festivals at

Sundance in Utah, *(http://festival.sundance.org)*, and Tribeca in New York City, *(www.tribecafilmfestival.com)*. You can also network and meet important contacts by volunteering. The website *www.shoots.com* has a complete list of festivals and film commissions. If you can, attend award shows and celebrity charity events as well.

Film Festival Volunteering

Sundance Film Festival
volunteers@sundance.org
Tribeca Film Festival
www.tribecafilmfestival.com
Cannes Film Festival
www.festival-cannes.org
Toronto International Film Festival
www.e.bell.ca/filmfest
Hamptons International Film Festival
www.hamptonsfilmfest.org
Maui Film Festival
www.mauifilmfestival.com
Urbanworld Film Festival
www.urbanworld.org
Monte-Carlo Film Festival
www.montecarlofilmfestival.com
Montreal Film Festival
www.ffm-montreal.org
Seattle Film Festival
www.seattlefilm.com

Happy celebrities Alec Baldwin and Maria Bello
at the Hamptons International Film Festival

Become a Celebrity Assistant

You can become a celebrity nanny or assistant. Stephanie
Birkitt ("Monti") is David Letterman's assistant who gained
fame from her many appearances on her boss's "The Late
Show." (Besides, you might get some great celebrity hand-
me-downs, invites, and freebies!) P. Diddy's valet and
personal assistant, Farnsworth Bentley, became famous when
pictured holding an umbrella for his boss in St. Tropez in July
2001. Since then he's appeared in a music video for OutKast
and in MTV's "Making the Band 2." One of his own songs
is on the group Da Band's debut album. He's developing a
comedy for Fox, and may become a Courvoisier spokesman.
Not too shabby for a former brollie holder, (*www.mr-bentley.
com*). Julie Roberts, not Julia, was an assistant to a Mercury
Records executive, who listened to her demo tape. Her self-
titled debut album was released in 2004, (*www.julieroberts.
com*).

Fran Drescher babysat for Twiggy's daughter in London and
her experience was the inspiration for the hit TV show "The

Nanny." When she happened to spot former president of CBS Entertainment Jeff Sagansky on an airplane, she knew she had him cornered. Before they landed a meeting was arranged in Los Angeles, and the rest is sitcom history.

Celebrity Personal Assistants, Inc.
www.celebritypersonalassistants.com
Association of Celebrity Personal Assistants
www.celebrityassistants.org

The music business is just as ruthless as Hollywood. Mariah Carey's story is legendary. She apparently went to an event with an audition tape, marched her way up to Tommy Mottola, the chairman of Sony Music, and handed it to him. He listened to it on the car ride home and the next thing you know, he signed her to her first recording contract and later married her. (*www.mariahcarey.com*).

Marilyn Manson, (*www.marilynmanson.com*), made flyers and brochures and passed them out at other bands' concerts. After the buzz he created Manson was eventually asked to perform live on local radio shows. Weird Al Yankovic, (*www. weirdal.com*), sent homemade tapes to the syndicated disc jockey, Dr. Demento, who played them. Before long Al had a record contract.

Do you know about music showcases? You never know if your new agent or record producer will be sitting in the crowd. You can find schedules for music showcases at *www.songwritershalloffame.org, www.ascap.com/about/ showcases.html*, and *www.bmi.com/showcases*. Want to write your own songs? *The Art of Writing Great Lyrics*, by Pamela Phillips Oland, can help you get started.

So get busy and be brazen. Show no fear. Remember, you are the moth to the spotlight that is fame. And above all, don't get discouraged. The more interesting and grueling the journey to fame, the better story it will make later when you're tearfully telling it to Barbara Walters.

•MUST DO•

Class picture-taking day is the most important day of the year! Hopefully you've been planning your claim to fame since high school, so make sure that your yearbook photos show how cute and naturally photogenic you were before you hit the big time. Get

a haircut, buy a new outfit, or even get a complete makeover. You can go to your local mall makeup counters -- a good one, of course, like Chanel, or a more basic one such as Prescriptives -- to get a free makeup application. Practice posing and smiling before you sit down in front of the camera. Your yearbook photos will surely wind up as one of E!'s "True Hollywood Trivia" questions at the movies, so make sure you look your best.

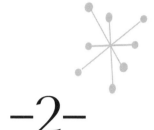

–2–

YOUR TEAM

"What is fame? The advantage of being known by people of whom you yourself know nothing, and for whom you care as little."
Lord Byron -- British Poet, 1788-1824

Now that you've received some recognition, you need a Fame 101 crash course on your handlers. You will need a manager, an agent, a personal assistant, a publicist, and a stylist, to name just a few.

Simply put -- the more people around you, the more loved you will feel and the more important you will look. Some tabloids have reported that J. Lo has roughly thirty-five people in her entourage. Apparently included in her team are not one, but two eyebrow specialists (one for each brow?), a hairdresser, color advisor, nipple tweaker, personal trainer, and a "life coach." <u>You</u> must know what the people working for you are supposed to be doing for you every second of every day. Their job depends on your fame, and your fame depends on them doing a good job.

•DID YOU KNOW?•

Life coaching celebrities has become a career option. A life coach can help people on a spiritual level, and also help them develop and achieve their career goals. Check out the Institute for Life Coach Training, *www.lifecoachtraining.com*. Visit the websites *www.inst.org/coach* and *www.reallifecoach.com* if you're interested in learning more. T.C. Conroy is a life-coach to the music and entertainment industry- helping rock bands is her specialty. www.westcoastcoaching.com

Managers vs. Agents

We don't want you to look like an amateur so it's imperative to know the difference between a personal manager and an agent. Managers guide your career and can also become producers and work on your projects. But agents and their firms can actually close the deals.

It's extremely glamorous to have both an agent and a manager and they should work together to make you as famous as possible. But if you have to choose, we recommend that you stick with a manager, even though he or she can take a much higher commission. Agents are state-licensed and can charge between 10% and 15%. Managers have their hand in everything because your career is their career. They are rarely bound to agency's and state rules, so they can usually charge what they like.

Got it?

Talent Agencies

Having a famous talent agency represent you is also very important. The Creative Artists Agency, otherwise known as CAA, (*www.caa.com*), and the William Morris Agency, (*www. wma.com*), are two of the best-known talent agencies in the business. Both are located in Los Angeles. Both have offices in New York.

Together these two agencies have clients such as Nicolas Cage, Gwyneth Paltrow, Pamela Anderson, John Travolta, Sandra Bullock, Faye Dunaway, and Salma Hayek. If you want to know what agent, manager or attorney represents which famous star, simply go to *www.whorepresents.com*.

Another place to look is in *The Hollywood Agents & Managers Directory*. However, you may want to check out smaller agencies, such as Catch 23 listed below. Their success depends on discovering the next best thing, and sometimes they're as hungry as you are.

Catch 23 Entertainment, Inc.
301 N. Canon Drive, Suite 207
Beverly Hills, CA 90210

Publicists

"There is no such thing as bad publicity, except your own obituary."
Brendan Behan -- Irish Playwright and Author, 1923-1964

Your publicist is a very important team member. He or she puts out your press releases and sets up your press junkets. Your publicist coordinates your book tour and signings and schedules your TV and radio appearances. He or she will also help you time your red carpet arrival perfectly and make sure you get into the right party or lecture circuit. Your publicist will get you on the cover of *Vanity Fair* and *People*, and your name in the newspapers and gossip columns. He or she will know all the important "celebrity wranglers" -- the people promoting the hot events, fundraisers, or charity events that you will need to attend. (At her 2005 Academy Awards Oscar-acceptance speech, Hilary Swank, at the last second, remembered to thank her "best friend and publicist." Not a bad idea to make sure your best friend is also the person you pay to say nice things about you to other people.)

However, when dealing with your publicist make sure to keep them in check. Not returning phone calls is the name of the game in Hollywood <u>only</u>. (It makes the person trying to reach you more intrigued by your unavailability.) But make sure they know which calls to return. You don't want to play hard-to-get with a Weinstein. Also, don't let your publicist be rude or obnoxious because they're having a bad day. Remember, they're representing you and your image. (And you should reconsider your situation if your PR person is getting more press than you are. *Lizzie Grubman, anyone?*)

•DID YOU KNOW?•

The Weinstein brothers, Bob and Harvey, named their company Miramax, (*www.miramax.com*), after their parents, Miriam and Max.

Top 10 television shows your
<u>publicist must get you on</u>

"TRL"
"The Oprah Winfrey Show"
"The Tonight Show with Jay Leno"
"The Late Show with David Letterman"
"Today"
"Entertainment Tonight"
"The View"
"Live with Regis and Kelly"
"Saturday Night Live"
"Charlie Rose"

Top 10 publications your
<u>publicist must get you in</u>

Vanity Fair
People
Teen People
US Weekly
Entertainment Weekly
TV Guide
Vogue
InStyle
Los Angeles Confidential Magazine
In Touch Weekly

When making television appearances, remember that red looks best. You can also wear blue and green, but primary colors look best. You might get away with wearing black or white but only if you're in the right light, so don't take that chance. <u>Never</u> <u>ever</u> wear stripes or checks. Also, unless you're a megastar like Tom Cruise at an award show, Mrs. Pete Sampras at the U.S. Open, Britney Spears trying to quit smoking, or a Major League baseball player, don't chew gum on camera. Mom was right -- you'll look like a cow.

PMK is the Los Angeles public relations firm for the über-famous. Pat Kingsley is the firm's founder and represents stars like Tom Hanks, Paris Hilton, Gwyneth Paltrow, Jennifer Aniston, Robert Redford, Matt Damon, Penelope Cruz, Jodie Foster, Russell Crowe, and until recently, Tom Cruise. (Cruise decided to go with his sister and fellow Scientologist, Lee Anne DeVette.) Kingsley's power is legendary in Hollywood and with entertainment magazine editors and journalists. Stan Rosenfield is another Hollywood publicist biggie who represents clients such as Robert De Niro, George Clooney, James Gandolfini, and Will Smith. Liz Rosenberg at Warner Bros. is the PR guru for Madonna, Liza Minnelli and Cher.

PMK/HBH
www.interpublic.com

Stan Rosenfield and Associates
2029 Century Park East
Los Angeles, CA 90067-2913

•DID YOU KNOW?•
You've really made it to the big time if you've made guest appearances on "Sesame Street," (*http://pbskids.org/sesame*), and "The Simpsons," (*www.thesimpsons.com*).

"Sesame Street" Guest Stars
Denzel Washington • 1989
Julia Roberts • 1991

Jim Carrey • 1993
Queen Latifah • 1993
Ellen DeGeneres • 1996
Jay Leno • 1998
Ben Stiller • 1999

"The Simpsons"
Aerosmith • 1991
The Ramones • 1993
Red Hot Chili Peppers • 1993
Meryl Streep • 1994
Rodney Dangerfield • 1996
Gillian Anderson and David Duchovny • 1997
Kelsey Grammer and David Hyde Pierce • 1997
Helen Hunt • 1998
Mark Hamill • 1998
Elton John • 1999
Burt Ward and Adam West • 2002
Tony Blair • 2003

10 Television Quotes

"Television! Teacher, mother, secret lover."
-- Homer Simpson

"Television: chewing gum for the eyes."
-- Frank Lloyd Wright

"Television has done much for psychiatry by spreading information about it, as well as contributing to the need for it."
-- Alfred Hitchcock

"I hate television. I hate it as much as peanuts. But I can't stop eating peanuts."
-- Orson Welles

"Americans will accept any level of mistreatment if they can get on television."
-- Bill Maher

"It's the American dream — being on TV!"
-- Kwame Jackson, "The Apprentice" runner-up

"Just because your voice reaches halfway around the world doesn't mean you are wiser than when it reached only to the end of the bar."
-- Edward R. Murrow

"Television is an invention that permits you to be entertained in your living room by people you wouldn't have in your home."
-- David Frost

"Television has proved that people will look at anything rather than each other."
-- Ann Landers

"Television: A medium — so called because it is neither rare nor well done."
-- Ernie Kovacs

The typical press junket will have you working non-stop, doing radio interviews, television and print interviews, book signings, one after the next. Make sure you like your publicist since you'll be spending an awfull lot of time with him/her. Remember there is a difference between the press and the paparazzi. You will covet the press and shun the paparazzi.

Good Publicity Lists

People magazine's "50 Most Beautiful People," "25 Most Intriguing People," "50 Most Eligible Bachelors," and "Sexiest Man Alive" -- *www.people.com*

Forbes "The Celebrity 100"
www.forbes.com/celebrity100/

Bad Publicity Lists

Mr. Blackwell's Worst-Dressed

The Razzies -- *www.razzies.com*

You don't want to wind up on the bad lists, but if you do, it's your publicist's job to put a positive spin on it.

•*DID YOU KNOW?*•

Brad Pitt was twice voted the "Sexiest Man Alive" by *People* magazine, in 1995 and 2000. He also made *People's* "Most Intriguing" and "Most Beautiful" issues as well.

•MUST DO•

No matter what -- be nice to the little people. Whether you're buying clothes, talking to a local journalist, or signing autographs in airports, you are your own best PR agent. You want the reputation of the nicest person in Hollywood.

Stylists

A personal stylist will cost you a small fortune, thousands of dollars a day, to keep your hair, makeup and overall image in top celebrity form. Some of the best stylists have their own managers as well. Sally Hershberger created Meg Ryan's razor-cut shag look and got a lot of mileage out of it. Because your stylist is your most important asset, you'll want to try and keep her a secret. You always want your fans to think you were born with good taste, great genes and naturally blond hair, so mum's the word. If you decide to dramatically change your look, proceed with caution. Keri Russell's short hairstyle caused a stir and was perceived to have negatively affected the ratings of "Felicity." So when your stylist wants to make a drastic change in your appearance make sure you run it by a focus group first. The website *www.seeing-stars.com/Shop/Hairdressers.shtml* is great for checking out hairdressers and salons to the stars, like the celebrity hairstylist José Eber on Rodeo Drive in Beverly Hills, *http://joseeberatelier.com*

•DID YOU KNOW?•

Chris McMillan created Jennifer Aniston's famous "Friends" haircut. You can visit his salon in Beverly Hills at 8944 Burton Way, 310-285-0088. (He's also reportedly the person whom Jennifer went to stay with after she and Brad split up.)

Phillip Bloch, *www.phillipbloch.com*, is known for styling A-list celebs like Jodie Foster, John Travolta, Sandra Bullock, Faye Dunaway, Halle Berry, Salma Hayek and Jessica Simpson. The list goes on and on. His new book *Elements of Style* offers help from this premiere Hollywood stylist.

Alexis Vogel, *www.alexisvogel.com*, has become famous for making up Pamela Anderson, Paula Abdul and "American Idol" Kelly Clarkson. This former emergency room nursing assistant has worked for *Playboy, Rolling Stone, Allure* and *Vogue*. Her smoky cat-eye glamour can be purchased on her website.

Laura Geller, *www.laurageller.com*, is another well-known makeup artist to celebs and top models. If you can't visit her New York studio, you can buy her products online and on the QVC channel, *www.qvc.com*.

•MUST DO•

Your look must be different every time your photo is taken. This means changing your hair and makeup every week. Here's an idea: keep your bangs long like Jennifer Aniston, Catherine Zeta-Jones, and Mischa Barton, so that way, with one quick brush to the side, you can change your look completely. We know it's exhausting work, but it's important to keep those fashion mags on their toes. Remember how supermodel Linda Evangelista changed her hair color what seemed like every other day! And Madonna was always reinventing her look.

•MUST DON'T•

Don't reinvent your look by gaining a ton of weight like Kirstie Alley. But if you pack on the pounds, do what she did -- get a comedy/reality TV show "Fat Actress" on Showtime, *(www.sho.com/site/fatactress)* and a spokesperson contract with Jenny Craig.

•MUST HAVE•

Are you too big of a celebrity to wash your hair by yourself? Aqua Vibro Automatic Shampoo Machine from Takara Belmont, *(www.takara-belmont.com)*, massages and cleans your head, all at the touch of a button.

Personal Chefs

Madonna and Oprah were the first to get us used to the concept of personal chefs. Let's face it -- your personal chef is really the only person who will be using your gourmet kitchen. They must be able to travel with you and know special macrobiotic recipes in case gal pals Gwyneth and Julia stop over for lunch. Peter Chaplin of Musical Knives, the award-winning vegetarian restaurant, toured with Madonna. Art Smith cooks for Oprah and wrote *Back to the Table: A Reunion of Food and Family*. Rosie Daley used to cook for Oprah, and published *In The Kitchen with Rosie: Oprah's Favorite Recipes*. They have cooked up a little fame of their own. (Inevitably, if you become famous, so will your personal chef.)

Personal Assistants

Your personal assistant should be recommended by another celebrity's personal assistant. Your assistant will take care of your household, pay your bills, screen your phone calls and fan mail, make appointments, and even plan your parties. Above all, your assistant will do your private errands, like discreetly running to the drugstore in the middle of night for your birth control and tampons and getting you the right kind of dressing on your salad or favorite brand of soymilk. He or she will know all your sizes (bras, dresses, suits, and shoes) and all your secrets and flaws. Make sure your assistant doesn't rob you blind or sell their story to the *National Enquirer* about your poor hygiene, temper tantrums and promiscuity. Make a contract with a no-blabbing (non-disclosure) clause, and have them sign a confidentiality agreement as a condition of their employment.

New York Celebrity Assistants

According to the New York Celebrity Assistants Website,

(*www.nycelebrityassistants.org*), this organization aims to "serve the unique needs of celebrity personal assistants in a confidential environment that is ultimately of mutual benefit to assistants and their celebrity employers." If your assistant isn't a member of this type of support group, then you're not working him hard enough. Make sure your assistant belongs to a celebrity assistant support group; they offer professional development, ways to network, job referral service, invitations to social events and much more.

David Malloy, David Spade's assistant, probably could have used this type of help. In the early morning hours he broke into Spade's home and tried to attack him with a stun gun. We don't want that to happen to you, so do a background criminal check on your new personal assistant. Hollywood power couple Will Smith and Jada Pinkett Smith reportedly had to file a restraining order against a former employee who allegedly threatened to disclose embarrassing allegations about the couple unless he was paid an enormous amount of money.

You always want to have a good relationship with your assistant, or you'll wind up on E!'s special "Revenge of the Celebrity Assistants," (*www.eonline.com/On/Special/RevengeCeleb*). You never want to find yourself in a messy lawsuit with your assistant/nanny, like Demi Moore and Bruce Willis.

•MUST DO•
Always be incredibly nice to other celebrity assistants because they're the ones holding the keys to the fort -- putting your calls through, and allowing access and entrance. Make sure your assistant knows other celebrity and other important muck-a-mucks assistants' birthdays. Send them presents

and flowers as much as possible. Chances are they're working so hard they deserve it anyway.

•MUST DON'T•

Fighting with your assistants is a major diva-don't. Naomi Campbell has been involved in legal battles with her assistants Georgina Galanis and Vanessa Frisbee. This never looks good, no matter how beautiful you are.

When picking your team, proceed with caution. Choosing the wrong member or combination could bring your career so far down that you'll be begging for an appearance on "Hollywood Squares" or even worse, filing for bankruptcy. Don't let that happen to you. You have to trust these people with your life and your money. You don't want to work this hard and fall from bling to bust as a result of a poorly timed tantrum.

Top 10 Bankruptcy Protection Filings

Kim Basinger • 1993

Gary Coleman • 1999

Anna Nicole Smith • 1996

TLC • 1995

Lorraine Bracco • 1999

Toni Braxton • 1998

Meat Loaf • 1983

Mike Tyson • 2003

Burt Reynolds • 1996

Planet Hollywood • 1999 and 2001

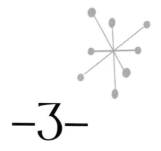

−3−

PREPARE THYSELF FOR SCRUTINY

"It's better to be looked over than overlooked."
Mae West -- American Actress, 1892-1980

It's not good enough to just be a celebrity -- you have to look like one. Your image is everything. Anna Wintour, the editor-in-chief of *Vogue* magazine, reportedly has her hairstylist come to her apartment every morning to blow-dry her bob pixie-straight, and gets professionally made-up.

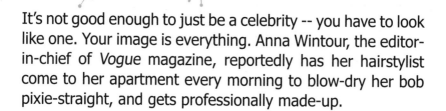

Among the gorgeous, famous, and female, showing skin is a competitive sport. The Grammy Awards has become the Mecca of the less-is-more believers. It's where J. Lo wore "the green dress" and Toni Braxton wore the white cutout loincloth dress by Richard Tyler. She's quoted as saying, "I figured before I get married and get pregnant, this is my moment to let it all go."

However, if you're going to let it all hang out like Toni, then you'd better be able to pull it off. You might want to decide what type of body you're looking for: the Jennifer Garner athletic look, rail thin like Jennifer Aniston, or curvaceous like Catherine Zeta-Jones and Jennifer Lopez. It's not a myth, the camera really does add 10 pounds.

Diet and Exercise

Carrie Wiatt created Diet Designs, *www.dietdesigns.com*, and touts Salma Hayek, Matt Damon and Dennis Quaid as clients. Demi Moore and Sting are reportedly fans of the raw food diet. Nothing gets heated above 118 degrees, except for their love lives. Jennifer Aniston, Cindy Crawford and Sandra Bullock supposedly balance their appetites with the Zone, *www.zoneperfect.com*.

Stay on top of the latest celebrity diets. Remember, whatever diet you choose, keep your personal chef in the loop. He or she will help you follow it and accomplish your goals. However, if you're a celebrity with a reputation for having an eating disorder it's critical for people to think that you're naturally thin because of a high metabolism. When eating out, especially with a journalist, you might want to order every course that's on the menu.

Kathy Kaehler is a "Today" show consultant, author of *Celebrity Workouts*, and celebrity personal trainer to stars like Julia Roberts, Cindy Crawford, and Michelle Pfeiffer. She has recommended walking and varying your workouts. In other words, to have a celebrity body you have to work very hard. We never said you could be fabulous *and* lazy.

Jennifer Lopez trains with Gunnar Peterson (above), *www. gunnarpeterson.com,* to get her spectacular body camera-ready. Halle Berry became "Catwoman" with the help of trainer Harley Pasternak, *www.harleypasternak.com.* Oprah and Bob Greene have made the connection. He's the fitness trainer, author of *Bob Greene's Total Body Makeover,* and guru who has Oprah lifting weights, running marathons, and eating less.

He's even helped McDonald's, *www.mcdonalds.com,* slim down with the Healthy Lifestyles Program, making Happy Meals healthier meals. Model/actor/Carolyn Bessette's former lover, Michael Bergin, works out at Billy Blanks Tae Bo studio.

Courteney Cox Arquette, Halle Berry, Liz Hurley, Kim Delaney, Sharon Stone, Jodie Foster, Sigourney Weaver, Jane Seymour, Jennifer Aniston, Charlize Theron, and Candice Bergen stretch our their spines and pump up with pilates. The list of celebrities who practice spiritually enlightening yoga, such as Sting, Demi Moore, Gwyneth Paltrow, Madonna, Ali MacGraw, Christy Turlington, and Diane Keaton is even longer.

•DID YOU KNOW?•

Actress Ali MacGraw put out the "Yoga Mind & Body" DVD, and supermodel and anti-smoking advocate Christy Turlington, *www.smokingisugly.com*, published *Living Yoga: Creating a Life Practice.*

Make sure you're up-to-date on the current celebrity workout trends. And whatever type of exercise religion you chose to follow, don't forget that one of your main goals is to make it into the British magazine *New Woman's* "Celebrity Bodies" section on a continuous basis, *www.newwoman.co.uk/health_beauty/celebrity_bodies/.*

•MUST DO•

When it comes to yoga, you mustn't look like an amateur. You have to know the different types. We've listed some of the most popular here although there are approximately 40 different kinds.

Types of Yoga
Anusura • A Hatha yoga system that celebrates the heart
Ashtanga • Most traditional and physically intense, this involves moving from pose to pose without stopping
Bikram • We call it sweaty yoga because the studio room's heated between 90 and 105 degrees
Ghata • synonym for Hatha
Hatha • yoga involving physical movement
Ivengar • named after B.K.S. Iyengar; sometimes called

"furniture yoga" and uses straps and cushions and blocks to help maintain yoga positions

Karma • based on cause and effect, and means, "to do," higher powers are important

Kripalu • founded by Amrit Desai, this is low-key yoga, holding positions longer to develop concentration and awareness

Kundalini • means "blissful energy," and is the least physically demanding

Mantra • we call this noisy yoga

Naya • similar to Hatha

Sivananda • meditation is important with this group

Viniyoga • words means "appropriate application" and can be less intense

Mark Blanchard is a yogi to the stars. He started progressive power yoga, *www.progressivepoweryoga.com*. Some of his celebrity clients include J. Lo, Teri Hatcher, Kim Delaney, Andy Garcia, Lucy Liu, and Drew Barrymore. He has produced workout videos to help you get started if you don't happen to live in Beverly Hills.

Gurmukh Kaur Khalsa is another yoga guru who teaches Kundalini yoga. She founded Golden Bridge Yoga in Los Angeles, *www.goldenbridgeyoga.com*, is the author of several books, and has been featured in *Vogue*, *InStyle*, and *The New York Times*.

•DID YOU KNOW?•

You can go on yoga retreats. The Kripalu Center for Yoga and Health, *www.kripalu.org*, is located in the Berkshires, and they offer 3-night healing retreats to renew your body. You can also take a yoga vacation on Paradise Island in the Bahamas with the Sivananda Yoga Retreat, *www.sivananda.org.*

Pilates

Don't know what Pilates is? Pilates is named after German-born Joseph Pilates in 1880. He trained as a boxer and gymnast and designed exercise equipment to help bed-ridden patients during World War I. He opened the first Pilates Studio in 1926. Ron Fletcher studied with Joseph and Clara Pilates and dancer/choreographer Martha Graham. He opened a studio in Beverly Hills and counts Ali MacGraw, Candice Bergen, and Steven Spielberg as converts. You can get his videos at *www.ronfletcherwork.com.*

Plastic Surgery

Plastic surgery has finally become acceptable. In fact, plastic surgeon Robert Kotler has just written *Secrets of a Beverly Hills Cosmetic Surgeon* and is one of the stars of E!'s "Dr. 90210," *www.eonline.com/On/Dr90210/.* Deborah Harry from Blondie admitted she had a facelift. Patricia Heaton from "Everybody Loves Raymond" told "Entertainment Tonight" she had a boob lift and wrote about her plastic surgeries in her tell-all book *Motherhood and Hollywood.* Janice Dickinson, a judge on "America's Next Top Model," wrote *Everything About Me Is Fake...And I'm Perfect.* Carol Burnett's chin implant was reported in the newspapers. Lawyer Greta Van Susteren, who became famous for analyzing the O.J. Trial, was open about the eyelift surgery she had before the premiere of her Fox News show, "On The Record."

Consider your plastic surgeon your new special friend. The much talked about Steven M. Hoefflin, MD, *www.hoefflin. com*, is based in Santa Monica, California and is a celebrity in his own right. He's known as the real "Doc Hollywood" and is rumored to have been a consultant for the movie.

Dr. Richard Fleming from Beverly Hills is another plastic surgeon to the stars. His website *www.bevhills.com* touts the institute as "well-known among Hollywood celebrities as the place for rejuvenating, subtle cosmetic surgery. Hollywood stars are frequent visitors."

Dr. Ricardo Lemos, *www.ricardolemos.med.br*, is the famous Brazilian plastic surgeon for the ultra-rich and super-private. Make no mistake about it -- plastic surgery isn't cheap. Breast enlargements can run you at least $3,000, a cleavoplasty $2,500, nose jobs over $7,000, face lifts up to $10,000, and lip augmentations $5,000. But don't be too discouraged. When you're famous your plastic surgery is a tax deduction. So is your personal trainer, by the way.

Types of Cosmetic Surgery
Blepharoplasty (otherwise known as eyelid surgery)
Botox
Cheek Augmentation
Chin Augmentation
Cleavoplasty
Collagen
Eyebrow and Forehead Lift
Facelift
Fat Transfers (lips, hands, laugh lines)
Liposuction
Rhinoplasty

Not quite!

Plastic Surgery Books
The Best Plastic and Reconstructive Surgeons – Christine Fullerton
Everything You Ever Wanted to Know About Plastic Surgery But Couldn't Afford to Ask – Alan Gaynor
Secrets of a Beverly Hills Cosmetic Surgeon – Robert Kotler
The Smart Woman's Guide to Plastic Surgery – Jean M. Loftus

•MUST DO•

Choose your plastic surgeon wisely. After all, this is an important decision. Make sure you check out the American Society of Plastic Surgeons, *www.plasticsurgery.org*.

Skin Deep

If you haven't been to sunny Brazil lately to visit plastic surgeon Dr. Lemos, don't worry. You can now get fake tans from the spa. The website *www.hollywoodtan.com* lists locations nearest you. To get the Mystic Tan procedure, go to *www.mystictan.com* -- "the official tan of the Dallas Cowboy Cheerleaders." Speaking of Brazil, get yourself a top-notch crotch. When in New York or South Beach, Florida visit the Brazilian J. Sisters International Salon, *www.jsisters.com/English/MainPageFramed.htm*, for the bikini wax of a lifetime. By the time you leave there won't be one unruly hair left on your body. Go to their website to see their "celebrity hall" -- a photo gallery of celebrity headshots and personalized celebrity thank-you notes.

•MUST GO•

Dr. Laurie Polis is a cosmetic dermatologist, *www.sohoderm.com*, and her list of celebrity clients reportedly includes Mel Gibson, Madonna, Drew

Barrymore, and models Kate Moss, Naomi Campbell, and Niki Taylor. New York City facialist Tracie Martyn, *www.traciemartyn.com*, uses electric currents to drain excess fluid and increase skin elasticity. Clients include Renée Zellweger and Liv Tyler, and it's rumored that Susan Sarandon and Tim Robbins go regularly for their $400 facials.

When in Beverly Hills, you can go the Sonya Dakar Skin Clinic, *www.soniadakar.com*, where all the A-list celebs go, such as Cameron Diaz, Drew Barrymore, Britney Spears, Kirsten Dunst, Debra Messing, Brittany Murphy, India Arie, Neve Campbell, and more.

•MUST DRINK•

Drinking plenty of water helps to keep skin looking great. Drink the water celebs Sting, Farrah Fawcett and Ellen DeGeneres reportedly drink -- Penta water, *www.pentawater.com*, the world's only patented purified water. Ryan O'Neal, Christopher Atkins, and athletes galore are listed as "Penta People" on its website. Bet you always wondered why the stars were 14% more hydrated than you.

Penta Drinkers

Christina Applegate	Steven Seagal
Celine Dion	Denzel Washington
Sean Penn	Robin Williams

Holy Water

If hard-core Kabbalists like Madonna get thirsty, they can drink sanctified water. The water can be personally blessed with the celeb's specific spiritual needs in mind. It can be ordered from the Kabbalah Centre, *www.kabbalah.com*

HOT
Sunscreen, microderm abrasions
and restalyne (which is also known as
the "new botox" and costs $500 a syringe)

NOT
Lip augmentation and Botox

There are many skin products that the stars use. Everyone from Patricia Heaton to Justin Timberlake has a skin routine.

Celeb Skin and Hair Care Products

Alterna Professional Haircare • *www.4alterna.com* for White Truffle Luxury Conditioner

Vida Emanuel • *www.vidaemanuel.net* for stronger more youthful skin

Epicuren • *www.epicuren.com* for professional enzyme skin treatment

Fred Segal Beauty • *www.fredsegalbeauty.com* the online beauty destination

GlyMed Plus • *www.glymedplus.com* for Cell Science Ultra Hydro Gel and age management products and vitamins

Ole Henriksen • *www.olehenriksen.com* for spa and products like the Rub n Buff Salt Scrub. Mr. Henriksen was a judge for the Miss Universe Pageant.

La Mer • *www.cremedelamer.com* for the crème de la crème

La Prairie • *www.laprairie.com* from Switzerland

Kanebo Cosmetics • *www.kanebo.com* from Japan, famous for the Sensai La Crème

Kinerase • *www.kinerase.com* for anti-aging and anti-wrinkles, and anti-cheap

Kinara • *www.kinaraspa.com* for Lactic Acid Hydrating Serum, to exfoliate nightly

Skin Medica • *www.skinmedica.com*, developed by dermatologists

Murad • *www.murad.com* for clarifying cleanser to fight acne

Wilma Schumann • *www.wilmaschumann.com* for acne and anti-aging products

SkinSimple • *www.skinsimpleonline.com* for Time Machine Line-Reducing Complex

Raising Eyebrows

When in Beverly Hills be sure to visit the self-proclaimed eyebrow king, Damone Roberts at his new salon *www. damoneroberts.com*. This eyebrow Michelangelo has sculpted some highbrow clientele like Madonna and Lara Flynn Boyle. Roberts is the star of the documentary "Star

Plucker," so go quickly, before the only chance you'll get to see him is at a Blockbuster near you. The other place celebs, like Renée Zellweger and Charlize Theron, go for their eyebrows is the Anastasia salon in Beverly Hills, www.anastasia.net/Salon.htm.

Body Art

Johnny Depp, Drew Barrymore, Britney Spears and Angelina Jolie all have tattoos. If you must get a tattoo the place to go is the Shamrock Social Club in Hollywood. Robert Downey, Jr. reportedly got his done there.

Mark Mahoney's Shamrock Social Club
9026 W. Sunset Boulevard, Hollywood, CA

Art to the Bone
13538 1/2 Ventura Boulevard, Sherman Oaks, CA 91423

•DID YOU KNOW?•

According to the American Society for Dermatologic Surgery, www.asds-net.org, over 50 percent of people with tattoos have considered removing them at one point or another, mostly because of career concerns, fading or outdated artwork, and the end of relationships, like Angelina Jolie. She had Billy Bob Thorton's name removed. Colin Farrell reportedly had part of his tattoo removed after his split with actress Amelia Warner. You can get laser tattoo removal, but there can be some scarring and it's actually more expensive than getting the tattoo put on in the first place. It can take six to ten sessions at a cost of $400 to $600 a visit. So think about this fashion trend carefully. If you really want a tattoo, remember -- black and red are the easiest colors to remove.

Eyeball jewelry is a fashion trend that has just hit the Netherlands. Dutch eye surgeons at the Netherlands Institute for Ocular Surgery, *www.niioc.nl*, have implanted eyeball jewelry, "JewelEye," in the mucous membrane. There's apparently a waiting list for the procedure. (Keep your eye on this one.)

Janet Jackson's nipple jewelry was reportedly made by Gauntlet for $120, but they're no longer in the boob business. If you're not exactly sure you want yours permanently pierced, try the temporary Nipple Huggers on for size, *http:// nipple-huggers.com*.

Fashion

The clothes you wear over your fabulous breasts are critical. They will be just as scrutinized as your body. A planned shopping trip to Rodeo Drive and the original Fred Segal complex at 8100 Melrose Avenue is a must. If you need some guidance, *www.seeing-stars.com/Shop/index.shtml* lists the stars' favorite salons, shops, shopping centers and malls, and boutiques. You can also look at the ads in *Vanity Fair* and *Vogue* to find out where you should be shopping.

•MUST GO•

Hot Los Angeles Shopping Districts

Beverly Boulevard	Sunset Plaza
Melrose Avenue	Rodeo Drive
Montana Avenue	Robertson Boulevard

Hot New York Shopping Districts

Madison Avenue

Soho

Sample sales are one way to get designer clothes at bargain prices. You can even plan your trip to New York City based on some of these hot sales. You can check out *www.nysale. com*, New York's Shopping Guide to Designer Bargains, and *www.clothingline.com* and *www.billiondollarbabes.com* to get exclusive e-mail invitations as to when and where these sales are held. Be prepared. These sample sales are breeding grounds for pandemonium. The website *www.dailycandy. com* is another place to check. You can subscribe for a free daily e-mail of the latest fashion and beauty if you live in New York, Los Angeles, or anywhere else for that matter. www. style.com is a must-visit website to find out what's hot on the runways, fashion show information and the latest news and trends. *www.overstock.com* has designer goodies for a lot less. And if you're really driven, you can go to the outlets in Secaucus, New Jersey and Freeport, Maine. The Burberry outlet alone in Maine is worth a trip up north. You can check out *www.premiumoutlets.com* to find outlet centers with stores and designers such as Barneys, Donna Karen, Hugo Boss, Kenneth Cole, Versace and more.

Recycling is another way to go. You can buy recycled or pre-owned designer clothing from celebrities, movie stars, socialites and the fashion elite. Maria Williams started *www. designerexposure.com*. She goes to the stars' homes and pays cash for their designer goods : Gucci, Gaultier, Chanel, Dior, Fendi, Hermès, Armani, Valentino, Versace, Vuitton, Chloe, Galliano, Dolce & Gabbana, Manolo Blahnik, and Jimmy Choo, to name a few. Now you can own them too.

Another place to check out for pre-owned celebrity clothes and accessories is *www.asos.com*. They also stock menswear fashions and sunglasses, jewelry, and even hair and beauty products.

Keep your eye on the auctions as well. From time-to-time Christie's, *www.christies.com*, and Sotheby's, *www.sothebys. com*, offer up the personal effects of Katharine Hepburn, Marilyn Monroe, John Lennon, and other celebrities. And you never know what you'll be able to find on *www.ebay. com*. At the Paper Bag Princess, *www.paperbagprincess. com*, stars find vintage couture gowns from Chanel, Dior, and Pucci. The store's owner, Elizabeth Mason, is also the author of *Valuable Vintage, The Insider's Guide to Pricing and Identifying Important Vintage Garments*.

•MUST DON'T •

Even if your career is in need of a publicity boost, don't resort to shoplifting. First of all, it's illegal and just because you might be an Academy Award Nominee doesn't mean you won't be prosecuted. You don't want to be associated with this crime forever. Have some control. Learn to browse through Bergdorf's, Saks, Bendel's and Barneys.

•MUST DO•

Only wear designers, or you'll look like a celebrity-in-crisis. Remember people are going to be constantly asking you what designer you're wearing, and you'll have to be able to respond in a respectful and appropriate manner. Dress only to impress.

•MUST GO•

Whether you're in London, Paris, Milan or New York City, twice a year in the fall and spring, you must sit in the front row of the runway shows during Fashion Week.

FASHION WEEK SCHEDULES

7th on Sixth

www.olympusfashionweek.com

London Fashion Week

www.londonfashionweek.co.uk

New York, Milan, Paris, London fashion week previews and events calendar

www.fashion-411.com/Fashion_Week.htm

News, designers, events, runway shows

www.fashionwindows.com

How you look while shopping is just as important. If you're a hip young star, wearing Juicy Couture sweatsuits and tracksuits, www.juicycouture.com, is very in right now. But please keep your eyes open for the next hot new sweatsuit, such as Yogini wear, www.myyogini.net, created by Debra Rodman.

•MUST DON'T•

Don't wear sneakers while shopping unless you have on a Juicy Couture sweatsuit at the time, or unless they're Reebok crocodile sneakers, which cost over

$1,000, *www.reebok.com/ltd*, or Pumas, *www.puma. com*. These sneakers have made a huge comeback and come in all different types of funky colors. Otherwise, only the elderly and tourists wear sneakers. You can spot tourists shopping in New York City from a million miles away because they wear sneakers with jeans (and usually have a bad perm job) -- big mistake!

Your jeans are just as important as your sweatsuit. You can try the higher-end stores like Barneys, Saks Fifth Avenue and Henri Bendel to find the top of the line hip-huggers the celebs wear from Bella Dahl, Mogg jeans, *www.moggjeans. com*, American Eagle Outfitters, *www.ae.com*, 7 for All Mankind, *www.sevenforallmankind.com*, and the 5-pocket jeans by James Jeans and Bartack.

IN

Tight and sexy, low-waist jeans.

OUT

Relaxed fit, really, really low-waist jeans.

Here's a trick: when the paparazzi snaps your photo as you walk down the street, make sure you're carrying a shopping bag from Gucci, Prada, Robert Cavalli, Pucci, or Chanel. You don't have to buy a lot -- a $200 shirt will do -- but get the bag. These shopping bags are part of your accessories for the day.

HOT

Cleavage -- boobs are back in. Since Janet Jackson's "wardrobe malfunction" it was bound to happen.

NOT

Midriffs -- we've all had enough of contemplating our navels.

TOP 10 DESIGNERS

Giorgio Armani	Richard Tyler
Roberto Cavalli	Giovanni Valentino
Oscar de la Renta	Donatella Versace
Christian Dior	Narcisco Rodriquez
Dolce & Gabbana	Tom Ford

FASHION QUIZ

1. Who designed J.Lo's green dress for the 2000 Grammy Awards?
2. Who designed Liz Hurley's dress to the premiere of *Four Weddings and a Funeral?*
3. Who did Andrew Cunanan murder in 1997 ?

4. Who has a famous sister who took over her brother's fashion empire after his death?

Anwer to all : Gianni Versace

Everything, we mean everything, you wear, makes a statement. Italian designers are great, but make sure to wear American designers when possible. It's just the patriotic thing to do right now. Besides, if you mix it up you'll have more designers offering their one-of-a-kind creations to you.

Carry a cup of designer coffee -- Starbucks will do. Renée Zellweger has been snapped a number of times carrying her cup of Starbucks. Even if you hate coffee, fill it with water and pretend. You'll appear as though it is no big deal for you to drop $5.00 on a cup of java as you walk through a store. And constantly talk on your cell phone. You want the media to think you're making an important deal with your agent or talking to your famous acting coach, Larry Moss, *www. larrymossstudio.com.*

Consider your shopping bags, beverage, and cell phone your main accessories, but if possible, you should also be carrying any products that you are currently endorsing. Don't make a big mistake and carry a can of Diet Coke if you're a Diet Pepsi spokesperson. This could cost you your job, especially if you're the princesses of pop, like Beyoncé Knowles and Britney Spears.

Celebrities <u>always</u> wear sunglasses. Have you ever seen Bono without them? But let us rephrase that -- designer sunglasses. Even if you are in a dark room, sunglasses are a must. Britney Spears and Tom Cruise have been spotted wearing Dior shades, Nicole Kidman has put on a pair of Prada, and Halle Berry has been known to wear Chloe. Brad Pitt's been seen in Calvin Klein Eyewear, Carrera's Huron shades by Safilo, Dior Homme, and the celebrity favorite, Oliver Peoples, *www.oliverpeoples.com*. Keanu Reeves' and Agent Smith's wraparound sunglasses designed by Blinde, *www.blinde.com*, can be found at *www.thematrixshop. com*.

IN

For the moment, aviator sunglasses are back in. Elle MacPherson and Jennifer Aniston are wearing this look. You can check it out at *www.rayban.com*

OUT

The extra-large Christian Dior sunglasses made famous by Paris Hilton.

•MUST HAVE•

You must have sunglasses and a baseball cap to wear when you're pretending to go incognito. Dark sunglasses are best, and your baseball cap should have nothing written on it, except if it's a baseball cap from your home team back in Cincinnati, for example. It's also a great look if you haven't been professionally made-up for the day. You can just put on lipstick, the hat, and glasses and nobody will know the difference.

The disheveled "I don't fuss about my appearance because I'm naturally fabulous" look is still in. When asked about your beauty secrets or products tell the press you only use Vaseline, Nivea, and Cherry ChapStick. But secretly have your personal assistant buy a $1,000 jar of La Mer. You can buy your Kinerase online at *www.drugstore.com.*

Your Smile

Many celebrities have had their teeth capped. If you don't want to go that far you can get your teeth professionally whitened. Dr. Vocaturo, the cosmetic dentist for the Miss USA and Miss Teen USA pageants has recommended the lumalight laser treatment, since it's quick and convenient, even if it's not cheap, costing as much as $1,000. But if you're on the road you can get the BriteSmile whitening gel, *www.britesmile.com,* or even Crest White Strips, *www. whitestrips.com*, will do if you're in a pinch. There's also Opalescence Tooth Whitening Systems, *www.ultradent. com.* And of course, there's the GoSmile Refillable Travel Compact, *www.gosmile.com.* Christie Brinkley, Chris Noth, and Eva Herzigova are listed as clients.

HOT
Listerine Oral Care Strips

NOT
Breath mints

—4—

CELEBRITUDE

"*Fame is a constant effort.*"
Jules Renard -- French Writer, 1864-1910

Your Speech

Celebrities make everything they say, especially the obvious or the simple, seem profound. In 1997, when singer Sheryl Crow was angry that Wal-Mart wouldn't sell her new album because one of the songs criticized the chain, she said bluntly, "I'm really p.o.'d about it." She then added, "I think that's in direct opposition to the First Amendment. People should stand up and say something about it." She made her subjective opinion sound like a universal belief. That's excellent celebrity speak!

And when film and TV writers threatened to strike in 2001, Warren Beatty said on CNN, "I think it would be very negative for the city, for the business, and for the companies, for the actors, for the writers, for the directors. It's not good at all."

He made the obvious seem profound and turned his opinion into a collective belief. That's the way to do it!

Top 10 Celebrity Expressions

"It's been a crazy, roller-coaster year."

"I can't wait to get back to the theater again."

"I signed on because of the director."

"Ultimately, it was all the traveling that ruined the relationship."

"I just try to live a very modest life."

"Can I be honest?"

"It's what I was into at the time."

"We separated over artistic differences."

"I needed more creative control."

"He/she is everything they say about him/her and more!"

THE ACTORS STUDIO

Practice your answers to the questionnaire James Lipton uses in case you're a guest on his show, "Inside The Actors Studio," *www.bravotv.com.* (L.A. The Actor's Studio, *left*)

Favorite word?
Least favorite word?

What turns you on?
What turns you off?
A sound you love?
A sound you hate?
Favorite curse?
Profession, other than your own, you most want to practice?
Profession you would not want to practice?
What you want God to tell you at the pearly gates?

When in public, sound as gracious and humble as possible. You never admit that you actually want to win an award. You're honored just to be nominated with the other extremely talented people in your category.

Top 10 Thank Yous

1. The Academy
2. Fellow Nominees
3. The Cast
4. Director
5. Agent
6. Manager
7. Producers
8. Parents (especially if they're deceased)
9. Family (spouse and kids)
10. God

•MUST DO•

Send your fellow nominees flowers. In fact, as a celebrity, you should constantly have your assistant send other celebrities flowers for their birthdays, or to wish them good luck when they get out of rehab. A special flower stylist should do the arrangement. Simon

Lycett is famous in England for his books on floristry and has arranged flowers for Elton John and the Queen Mother. Closer to home, Rodney Dangerfield's widow owns a flower shop that all, we mean all, the celebrities use. At the website *www.jungleroses.com*, you'll see a celebrity-clientele list of over 100.

•MUST BORROW•

You must borrow your jewelry from Harry Winston, *www.harry-winston.com*, when attending award shows.

Harry Winston Wearers

Julie Andrews • diamond cluster earrings, 5-carat necklace

Selma Blair • ruby and diamond ring, diamond stud earrings

Helena Christensen • million-dollar diamond necklace, diamond bracelet

Billy Crystal • sapphire and crystal studs, cufflinks

Faith Hill • necklace, ring, earrings and bracelet

Diane Lane • 22-carat diamond ring, 6-carat diamond earrings

Lucy Liu • diamond earrings, turquoise and gold bracelet, ring

Jada Pinkett Smith • diamond earrings

Gwen Stefani • diamond and pearl brooch, diamond bracelet, diamond stud earrings, diamond ring

Sting • 3-carat diamond stud earring

•DID YOU KNOW?•

Brad Pitt's a jewelry designer. He partnered with Giorgio Damiani to create the D. Side line, *www.damiani.com*.

•MUST HAVE•

Celebrities have pets. Leonardo DiCaprio, Charlize Theron, Helen Hunt, Gwen Stefani, Oprah Winfrey, Edie Falco, K.D. Lang and Paris Hilton all own dogs. Christopher Ameruoso wrote *Pets and Their Celebrities* so you can get some ideas as to which pet you should own. He'll also take your pet's headshot should you decide to get Rover into the business. Make sure your pet is small enough to carry around as you stroll through Bergdorfs and Saks and can travel with you. Don't worry -- your assistant will walk it. And do the right celebrity thing -- buy your pet a cemetery plot. In Hollywood, the place to go when your pooch passes away is the Los Angeles Pet Memorial Park, *www.lapetcemetery.com*. The pets of Steven Spielberg, Bob Newhart, Diana Ross, Charlie Chaplin and Humphrey Bogart are supposedly buried there. If you live in New York it's the prestigious Hartsdale Pet Cemetery and Crematory, *info@petcem.com*. Elizabeth Arden, former New York City Mayor Jimmy Walker, and the bandleader Xavier Cugat have put their pets to rest here.

The Official Celebrity Handbook Pet Quiz

1. What was the name of Joan River's dog?
2. What's the name of Paris Hilton's Chihuahua?
3. What was the name of President Bill Clinton's dog that was hit by a car?
4. What's the name of George Clooney's pet pig?
5. What are the names of Kathie Lee Gifford's dogs?

(Answers: Spike, Tinkerbell, Buddy, Max, Chardonnay, Chablis and Regis.)

Bo Derek, Patrick Swayze, James Woods, Ted Turner, and Robert Wagner are just a few celebrity horse fans. Bruce Springsteen's daughter, Jessica, is an equestrian. Christie Brinkley and family can usually be seen annually at the Hampton Classic in the summer, *www.hamptonclassic.com*. In the celebrity world, owning horses shows that you're well-bred and environmentally sensitive.

•*Did You Know?*•

In 1998, California's initiative, *www.savethehorses.com*, to ban horse slaughter was supported by Robert Redford, Paul and Linda McCartney, Diane Keaton, Pierce Brosnan, Stephanie Powers, Dyan Cannon, Peter Falk, Carroll O'Connor, Brigitte Bardot, Malcolm McDowell, Keeley Shaye Smith, Kevin Nealon, Roy Clark, Sophie B. Hawkins, Martina Navratilova, Linda Blair and Tippi Hedren.

Your Crib

Choosing where to live can be tricky. You have to find the right city for your star to shine. If you've decided to become a blockbuster Miramax celebrity, and are still young enough to try, we recommend you move to Los Angeles. If you want to be a famous artist or writer, or be taken as a serious actor, then New York City is the place for you.

•*Did You Know?*•

Did you know that approximately 70 percent of the low-rent apartments in the Manhattan Plaza building at 43rd and Ninth Avenue are reserved for stagehands, composers, dancers, choreographers, makeup artists, stand-up comics, and actors? There's a 10-year waiting list and to qualify at least 50 percent of your income for the last three years must come from working in the performing arts. Oakwood, "the entertainment housing specialists," *www.oakwood.com*, rents to people in the entertainment industry.

Make no mistake about it -- where you live in these cities is crucial. While trying to make it as an actor, make sure your address has a Beverly Hills, West Hollywood, Malibu, or Encino zip code, even if you have to live above a garage. You'll need that posh address when your manager is sending out your CV with photo. You want to appear as though you have plenty of money and can do with or without that acting job. New York City provides a bit more flexible in this territory. If you're a hot new star you have to live in the Village. If you're a seasoned celebrity it's important to appear that you crave anonymity and therefore will only live on the Upper West Side. Frances McDormand and Kyra Sedgwick and Kevin Bacon live there. Woody Allen and family are East Siders. If you're a celebrity-in-crisis and need extra media attention, quickly move to London (or get pregnant).

If you're known for your political commentary or entangle-ments, you must live in the Washington area. If you're a Democrat, you've got to have a Georgetown townhouse. If you're a Republican, then move to a mansion in McLean, Virginia. If you're politically incorrect, the Watergate Apartments, *www.watergatedc.com*, might be the right place for you.

•MUST DO•

When buying a house in California, buy the most expensive multi-million dollar home you can afford, just to get the land. Once you own the property, tear down the house and build your own home.

Price is no object. If you like the beach, Malibu is for you; for city views, move to the Hollywood Hills and if you need a mega-mansion, Beverly Hills, Brentwood, or Bel Air might just be your 'hood.

If you're Australian you must keep a ranch down under to escape to when the pressures of Hollywood become too much. You'll also want to become an ambassador to the Australians in Film organization, *www.australiansinfilm.org* and a member of the Australian Film Commission, *www.afc.gov.au.*

Famous Aussies

Cate Blanchett	Naomi Watts
Bryan Brown	Geoffrey Rush
Toni Collette	Guy Pearce
Russell Crowe	Olivia Newton-John
Mel Gibson	Heath Ledger
Hugh Jackman	Nicole Kidman

"The Trash"

It's important to publicly state that you pay no attention to what is written about you in those "trashy" supermarket tabloids. However, be careful when you make that statement. Double-check that you're not actually suing the *National Enquirer* at that exact moment. Otherwise it's embarrassingly obvious how much you scrutinize the same publication you claim not to read.

•MUST DON'T•

Before you run off and sue the tabloids, make sure what they write isn't actually true! Halle Berry said that she was going to sue a tabloid for writing about her now ex-husband Eric Benet's reported cheating, but then he finally confessed that it was true. Halle Berry made no secret of the fact that the tabloids had it right!

•*DID YOU KNOW?*•

Attorneys for Cody Gifford, son of celeb parents Katie Lee and Frank, filed a defamation suit in 2000 when Cody was only 10 years old, claiming that the *National Examiner* fabricated stories of Cody's alleged bad temper and misbehavior. You're never too young to set the tabloids straight. Ashley Olsen filed a $40 million lawsuit against the *National Enquirer* for defamation pertaining to a story they ran in early 2005 about an alleged drug scandal.

Biggest Tabloids

British
Daily Express
www.express.co.uk
Daily Mirror
www.mirror.co.uk
Daily Star
www.dailystar.co.uk
The Sun
www.thesun.co.uk
News of the World
www.newsoftheworld.co.uk

American
The National Enquirer
www.nationalenquirer.com
Globe Magazine
www.globemagazine.com

National Examiner
American Media, Inc., 1000 American Media Way, Boca Raton, FL 33464
Star
www.starmagazine.com
Weekly World News
www.weeklyworldnews.com

•DID YOU KNOW?•

The *Daily Mirror* apologized and its editor, Piers Morgan resigned after printing fake photos of alleged abuse of Iraqi soldiers by British troops. The tabloid says it believed the photos were genuine at the time of publication.

Book Smart

Be sure to memorize the number four or five book on *The New York Times* non-fiction bestsellers list. That way if a journalist asks what book you're currently reading you stand a better chance that the journalist hasn't read that one yet. Also, have a copy of *Pride and Prejudice* and *Leaves of Grass* on you whenever possible. If you're a celebrity sports figure, carry the Bible with you at all times.

Top 10 Suggested Books to Carry

Pride and Prejudice – Jane Austen
Kabalah for a New Millennium: A Guide for Spiritual Growth – Tulia Rikles-Osta
Ulysses – James Joyce
Leaves of Grass – Walt Whitman
An Actor Prepares - Constantine Stanislavski
The Road Less Traveled – M. Scott Peck
The Dalai Lama's Book of Wisdom – Dalai Lama

The Celestine Prophecy – James Redfield
The Fountainhead – Ayn Rand
Crime and Punishment – Fyodor Dostoevsky

IN
Film and Kabbalah clubs

OUT
Book and dining clubs

Traveling

When it comes to traveling, nothing compares with charter planes. We recommend Trans-Exec Private jets, *www. transexec.com*. If you're not famous enough to fly by charter, you must always fly first class, preferably between New York and Los Angeles, at least every other month. Make sure your publicist leaks that you'll be arriving at LAX on the 4 pm flight so the paparazzi can snap a shot of you walking through the airport with your sunglasses on. After LAX, the second most important airport to be seen at is London's Heathrow. This signals to the head honchos that you're an international celebrity as well.

•MUST HAVE•

Your luggage and handbag reflect your celebrity status. You can visit Beverly Hills Luggage, *www.beverlyhillsluggage.com*, and *www.eluxury.com* for a wide selection of designer bags.

Handbags and Luggage

Il Bisonte
www.ilbisonte.com
Chanel
www.chanel.com to find a boutique near you for the
multipocket Cambon bag
Hermès
www.hermes.com to order the custom-made,
wait-listed Birkin bag
Sigerson Morrison
www.sigersonmorrison.com
Mulholland Brothers
www.mulhollandbrothers.com
Tumi
www.tumi.com
Valextra
www.valextra.com
Louis Vuitton
www.vuitton.com

•MUST STAY•

Los Angeles

Chateau Marmont (right)
www.chateaumarmont.com
Regent Beverly Wilshire
www.regenthotels.com
Beverly Hills Hotel
www.beverlyhillshotel.com
Mondrian
www.mondrianhotel.com
Hotel Bel Air
www.hotelbelair.com

New York

W
www.whotels.com
Rihga Royal
www.rihgaroyalny.com
Tribeca Grand
www.tribecagrand.com
The Carlyle
www.thecarlyle.com

Washington, D.C.

Ritz-Carlton
www.ritzcarlton.com
Relais Chateaux Morrison House
www.morrisonhouse.com
Hay-Adams
www.hayadams.com

London

Le Meridien
www.lemeridien.com
The Carlton Tower
www.carltontower.com
The Dorchester
www.dorchesterhotel.com
Claridge's
www.claridges.co.uk
St. Martins Lane Hotel
www.morganshotelgroup.com
Milestone Hotel and Apartments
www.milestonehotel.com

·MUST HAVE·
In your hotel and dressing rooms make sure there

are copious bottles of Evian and Cristal, as well as any other beverages or foods, that you've requested through your agent, like frozen M&M's if you're Bryant Gumbel, or only green ones or no green ones, or Smarties if you're Venus Williams. If they bring you Poland Spring or cheaper brands of champagne like Moet, or peanut instead of plain, you should keep complaining until you get what you want. You can check out www.thesmokinggun.com/backstagetour, to see contracts of what special accommodations and meals celebrities like the Rolling Stones, Britney Spears, Jennifer Lopez, Mariah Carey, Sting, and the Backstreet Boys require in their dressing rooms.

HOT
Vitamin Water cocktails and martinis

NOT
Cosmopolitans and apple martinis

•MUST BE SEEN•

Los Angeles

Beauty Bar • *www.beautybar.com*, 1638 North Cahuenga Boulevard, 323-464-7676, The place to get a manicure and henna hand tattoos, so you'll look great holding that drink in this vintage beauty salon/glamour establishment.

Forty Deuce • *www.fortydeuce.com*, 5574 Melrose Avenue, 323-465-4242, It's seductive and sexy and where Jessica Simpson threw husband Nick Lachey's 30th birthday party.

Joseph's Café • *www.josephscafe.com*, 1775 N. Ivar Avenue, 323-462-8697, They've made Greek chic. Drink and dance 'til dawn.

The Roxy • 9009 Sunset Boulevard, 310-278-9457, It's one of L.A's top music clubs and a showcase for up-and-coming talent. Keep this in mind.

Sky Bar • *www.mondrianhotel.com*, 8440 Sunset Boulevard, 323-650-8999, Very exclusive and the best view of the city. Maybe you'll see some models/waitresses.

The Standard Roof Bar • 550 S. Flower Street, 213-892-8080. There's an outdoor pool and lounge party.

Star Shoes • 6364 Hollywood Boulevard, 323-462-STAR, It's unique because it's a vintage shoe store and bar – very trendy.

The Viper Room (left)• *www.viperroom.com*, 8852 Sunset Boulevard, 310-358-1881, Yes, we all know that it was owned by Johnny Depp, and the River Phoenix story.

Whisky A Go Go • *www.whiskyagogo.com*, 8901 Sunset Boulevard, 310-652-4202. It's still the place where rock bands hope to make it big, a la Jim Morrison and The Doors, Janis Joplin and Led Zeppelin.

New York

Suite 16 • 127 Eighth, 212-627-1680, 16 banquette booths with mini-bars, the place for the beautiful people who make it on the guest list.

40/40 • 6 W. 25th Street, 212-989-0040. It's Jay-Z's new sports bar.

Suede • 161 W. 23rd Street, 212-633-6113, It's the place for the beautiful, hip and trendy. It's where Jamie-Lynn DiScala was given her 23rd surprise birthday party.

Spirit New York • 530 W. 27th Street, 212-268-9477, Separate floors designated for the mind, body and soul for the hip and single.

•MUST EAT•

Los Angeles

Blowfish Sushi to Die For • 9229 Sunset Blvd., 310-887-3848. Where Lindsay Lohan celebrated her 18th birthday.

Mr. Chow • www.mrchow.com, the place to see and be seen.

Dolce • 8284 Melrose Avenue, 323-852-7174. Celebrity owned.

Le Dome Restaurant • 8720 Sunset Boulevard, 310-659-6919. Have your power lunch here and meet your newest celebrity mate.

KOI • www.koirestaurant.com, 730 North La Cienega Blvd., 310-659-9449, Japanese Mecca, but your order won't get lost in translation.

Morton's • *www.mortons.com*, 435 S. La Cienega Blvd., 310-246-1501, Steakhouse chain and favorite in Beverly Hills.

Rainbow Bar and Grill • *www.rainbowbarandgrill.com*, 9015 Sunset Boulevard, 310-278-4232

New York

Elaine's •1703 2nd Avenue, 212-534-8103

Flow • 150 Varick Street, 212-929-9444, Flowing upstairs water bar.

The Four Seasons • *www.fourseasonsrestaurant.com*, 99 East 52nd Street, 212-754-9494 Designed by famous architect Philip Johnson. You might see supermodels.

Fresco by Scotto • *www.frescobyscotto.com*, 34 E. 52nd Street, 212-935-3434, Harrison Ford, Regis Philbin, Katie Couric, Matt Lauer, and Jennifer Aniston have all reportedly eaten here.

Michael's • *www.michaelsnewyork.com*, 24 West 55th Street, 212-767-0555, Where you'll find former Presidents, and media and publishing celebs.

Nobu • *www.noburestaurants.com*, 105 Hudson Street, 212-219-0500, Robert De Niro's a partner -- expensive but yummy.

The Whiskey Blue • *www.whotels.com*, 541 Lexington Avenue, 212-755-1200, Part of the chic W Hotel

•DID YOU KNOW?•

The restaurant Elaine's is a New York Upper East Side institution. It started as a haven for writers and became the place to see and be seen. Here you might mingle with Woody Allen, Joan Rivers, or Jack Nicholson. It all depends on the night. You can find out more about Elaine's and the owner Elaine Kaufman in A.E. Hotchner's book, *Everyone Comes to Elaine's*. When you go, just make sure they don't lead you to the left side of the restaurant against the wall. Rumor has it that's where the nobodies are seated.

Some Celebs Who Have Dined and Dished at Elaine's:

Ellen Barkin	Sean Connery
Mikhail Baryshnikov	Clint Eastwood
Peter Boyle	James Gandolfini
Marlon Brando	Dusting Hoffman
Michael Caine	Mick Jagger
Jackie Kennedy	Frank Sinatra
Larry King	Sylvester Stallone
Calvin Klein	Sharon Stone
Chris Noth	Barbra Streisand
Gwyneth Paltrow	Elizabeth Taylor
Arnold Schwarzenegger	Paul Simon

•MUST DO•

Your birthday party has to be the celebrity event of the year. You can have it at any of the places listed above, but if possible, it should be underwritten. Naomi Campbell reportedly celebrated her 34th in St. Tropez in grand style with the help of sponsors Cirque du Soleil and Alfa Romeo.

If you're going to have your birthday party at home, you can rent state of the art portable toilets at *www.andygump.com*. These luxury potties include flat screen TV's and wall-to-wall carpeting. (After all, you don't want people rooting through your bathroom cabinets.)

Your Cars

What you drive matters almost as much as your appearance and where you hang out. Two cars, a Range Rover and a

Home on the celebrity Range

Jaguar, are a must for any ultra-celebrity couple like Courteney and David. The Range Rover signifies that you're on the go and adventurous, all the while retaining a shred of practicality. This is considered the station wagon of the famous. The Jaguar shows that you have taste, style and class. If you're looking to give your celebrity status a little lift, drive something gaudy -- a Bentley will do. If you're confident in your celebrity status, you can give up the posh leather seats and tool around in a hybrid car. This will show that you care more about the environment than showing off.

Top 10 Hybrid Car Fans

Ed Begley, Jr.
Ted Danson
Larry David
Cameron Diaz
Leonardo DiCaprio

Arianna Huffington
Calista Flockhart
Harrison Ford
Rob Reiner
Tim Robbins

•DID YOU KNOW?•

According to the automotive information company R.L. Polk & Co., more Americans are buying hybrid cars because of higher gas prices and newer hybrid models. Honda has a hybrid Civic and is introducing a hybrid version of its Accord this year, *www.hondacars.com*. Toyota has the Prius, *www.toyota.com/prius*. Ford is coming out with hybrid version of its Escape sports utility vehicle, *www.fordvehicles.com/escapehybrid*. Lexus is also planning a hybrid SUV, *www.lexus.com/models/hybrid*.

If you're a celebrity residing in New York, it's a different story. You'll need a driver and this year you must be seen in a Mercedes S500 with blacked out windows. Last year it was the Chevy Suburban with blacked out windows. In general, when in New York, the car should always have blacked out windows. But if you are worried that you won't be able to keep up with this latest car-changing trend, then ride in a brand new Lincoln Town Car. It's a timeless classic -- you can't go wrong.

IN
The Lincoln BPS (Ballistic Protection Series), *www.lincoln.com*, is bullet-proof. Hey, we live in crazy times, you never know.

OUT
The Hummer, *www.hummer.com*. We may live in crazy times, but gas ain't cheap.

•MUST DO•
Take a driving or racing class at the Harvard of

auto colleges, Skip Barber Racing School, *www. skipbarber.com*. This will help you avoid the paparazzi, drive like a pro, and help you qualify for the Toyota Pro/Celebrity Race, *www.toyota.com*.

•DID YOU KNOW?•

When in California, you can rent your dream car. No one will know it's not yours when you show up for your audition or photo shoot. Beverly Hills Rent-a-Car, *www.bhrentacar.com*, rents any exotic car your heart desires. So when you pull up at the red carpet at top speed, that Maserati Spyder GT will look like yours.

•MUST HAVE•

You should be the first celeb to have a car brand named after you. Can you imagine all the women who would be driving an Oprah down the road if it were on the market, or all the guys who'd like to be cruising along the highway in a Jeter?

YOUR TRAILER

When it comes to your trailer, the bigger the better. The actor Lyle Waggoner created Star Waggons, *www.starwaggons. com*. He claims John Travolta as a big customer. Make sure your manager gets one of his trailers in your contract. If you're a pop star, you must travel in a tour bus with style. It must be equipped with a tanning bed, laundry facilities, a stripper pole, Playstation and flat-screen TV.

–5–

MONEY, MONEY, MONEY

"To become a celebrity is to become a brand name."
Philip Roth -- American Writer

As a celebrity you need to become a brand, so you will still be able to cash a few checks if your career heads south. (Keep this in the back of your mind while making important business decisions. You may want to say yes to doing commercials in Japan or England, for example, even if it's an idea or product that your manager or agent would otherwise nix.)

•*DID YOU KNOW?*•

Brad Pitt has done ads for Edwin Jeans, *www.edwin-jeans.com*, and coffee in Japan. While Jennifer Aniston has made ads for the Barclaycard credit card, *www.barclaycard.co.uk*, in England.

Branding

To become a brand your name must be associated with something that sells. George Foreman will forever be linked with his grilling machines. The Olympic skier Suzy Chaffee is better known as Suzy ChapStick. The easiest way for you to do this is to find your own trademark. If you're an actor, find a movie role that will sell your character (your face) over and over again. Harrison Ford is known for his trademark role as Indiana Jones. Keanu Reeves is the face of The Matrix. Tony Hawk is a skateboarder and the face of Sony's Pro Skater videogames, *www.activision.com*. Actress Julianne Moore's trademark is her red hair, and she's made the most of it in a Revlon commercial for hair color. Halle Berry is also a Revlon woman, *www.revlon.com*. Catherine Zeta-Jones has made talking on cell phones sexy. She's the global spokeswoman for T-Mobile, *www.t-mobile.com*, and is getting plenty for it. Jerry Seinfeld and Superman will forever be associated with American Express, *www.americanexpress.com*. Old Navy, *www.oldnavy.com*, commercials are breathing life into the careers of Morgan Fairchild, Erik Estrada and Joan Collins.

Infomercials

Do not underestimate the power of the infomercial. Although it may seem that it's for B-list celebrities only, an infomercial is free advertising for you -- hopefully, when you need it most. Maybe Judith Light had nowhere to go after playing the mom on the hit 80s show "Who's the Boss?" but she endorsed the skin care line Proactiv, *www.proactiv.com*, and is logging some great face time of her own on Sunday afternoons and keeping her plugged into the celebrity community.

Fitness infomercials are especially popular. Who would have thought that Suzanne Somers, a Farrah Fawcett-wannabe, and sexy star of "Three's Company," would be squeezing her thighs on national television? But her name recognition from doing those Thigh Master infomercials added greater intrigue when she came out of the plastic surgery closet. And then she made even more money by writing a book to explain it all. No shame, no gain. Carmen Electra has come out with the aerobic striptease, *www.aerobicstriptease.com.* Elizabeth Filarski Hasslebeck is the spokeswoman for Tae Bo, *www.billyblanks.com.* Daisy Fuentes promotes Winsor Pilates, *www.winsor-pilates.net.* Zora Andrich from "Joe Millionaire" lost weight with Nutrisystem, *www.nutrisystem. com.* And of course, there's bosomy Anna Nicole Smith, who lost weight but gained money with Trimspa, *www.trimspa. com.*

Clothing and products are another way to go. Jessica Simpson advertises Dessert fragrances, makeup and bath treats, *www.dessertbeauty.com* and *www.sephora.com*, and is the acne-free face of Proactiv, *www.proactiv.com.* The name Jaclyn Smith will forever be a household name due to her clothing line at Kmart, while the career of Kate Jackson, another former Charlie's Angel, has virtually faded into the sunset. J. Lo has perfume, clothes, music, and who knows -- she'll probably have her own magazine next. Always keep in mind that you need to be advertising yourself no matter where your career goes.

Celebrities with Clothing Lines

Christy Turlington
http://nuala.puma.com
Elle Macpherson
www.figleaves.com
Jennifer Lopez
www.jenniferlopez.com

Kathy Ireland
www.kathyireland.com
Mary-Kate and Ashley Olsen
www.marykateandashley.com and *www.walmart.com*
Emme
www.officialemme.com
Sean "P. Diddy" Combs
www.seanjohn.com
Eminem
www.shadyltd.com
Jaclyn Smith
www.jaclynsmith.com

Celebs with Perfumes

Scarlett Johannson • Calvin Klein Eternity
www.sephora.com
Nicole Kidman • Chanel No 5
www.chanel.com
Jennifer Lopez • Glow by J. Lo
www.shopjlo.com
Britney Spears • Curious
www.britneyspearsbeauty.com
Celine Dion Parfums
www.cotyshop.com
Donald Trump the Fragrance
www.trump.com
Mary-Kate and Ashley Olsen
www.cotyshop.com

Restaurateur

Become a celebrity restaurateur. Rob Morrow, Dr. Joel Fleischman from "Northern Exposure," opened the healthy, dairy-free *Josie's Restaurant and Juice Bar* in Manhattan, *www.josiesnyc.com*, in 1994 and 10-plus years later it's still packing them in. However, if you're going to be associated with a restaurant, make sure you know what you're doing. The restaurant business is very dicey. Britney Spears was associated with and then disassociated with the troubled restaurant *Nyla*. Steven Spielberg and Jeffrey Katzenberg launched the theme restaurant *Dive*, but it tanked in 1999. However, Spielberg's mom's kosher restaurant, Leah Adler's *The Milky Way*, is doing great. We're not even going to mention *Planet Hollywood*, but J.Lo's restaurant *Madre's* in Pasadena, (*www.madresretaurante.com*), apparently has quite a waiting list.

•DID YOU KNOW?•

Mary-Kate Olsen says that she's interested in cooking and wants to attend culinary school. Um, are there restaurant possibilities to add to the Olsen's billion-dollar empire? Keep this in mind -- true brands are always thinking. In fact, the band Kiss even came up with the Kiss Kasket. In 2001, over 2,000 Kiss Kaskets went on sale for $5,000 a pop on *www.kissonline.com*. Now that's covering all your brand bases from head to toe.

But speaking of going under, if you're going to do an erectile dysfunction commercial, you have to be extra secure in your manliness. Mike Ditka is the spokesman for Levitra, and Bob Dole will be forever linked with Viagra. They're obviously comfortable with being associated with sexual dysfunction products. After all, who's going to pick on them?

Rosie O'Donnell, the gun-control advocate, did Kmart commercials, then resigned as their celebrity spokeswoman because the chain store stocked ammunition and hunting rifles on its shelves. Make sure your assistant does her homework before you sign up as a spokesperson.

A good fan club and website are easy to accomplish -- that's what interns are for. Just employ someone responsible to oversee both and have some kids send out the goods. Faith Hill used to work for Reba McEntire's fan club before she started on her own. It's important that you register your name for your website now, even if you aren't a hot new celebrity yet. This will save you from an annoying lawsuit when you try to get it back later. Sell your goods on the website -- CDs, posters, coffee mugs, and even Christmas ornaments. Nothing is too outrageous.

•MUST DO•

Stake your claim in cyberspace right now. Cyber squatters are known for holding websites hostage by registering the names of celebrities and then asking for ransoms to get them back. Madonna filed a complaint against Dan Parisi, who registered the domain name *www.madonna.com* for his porn website. Lucky for the Material Girl, she was already "the owner of U.S. Trademark Registrations for the mark MADONNA for entertainment services and related goods." The World Intellectual Property Organization, *www.wipo. int* agreed Parisi registered the domain name in "bad faith" and ruled that he relinquish the domain to Madonna. Julia Roberts, Led Zeppelin, Jethro Tull, and Tina Turner were able to get their domain names back too. Who says there's no celebrity justice?

•MUST DON'T•

If you're a "lifestyle icon" (an icon of sport, fashion and family values, and brand name), whatever you do, don't cheat on your famous spouse. This could be bad for your marketing potential and your brand name. European tabloids are speculating on an alleged affair between Beckham and his former personal assistant, Rebecca Loos. The Beckham brand is valued at approximately $370 million largely due to endorsements from PepsiCo, Vodafone, Marks & Spencer, Siemens, and Adidas. If the press is speculating about your alleged affairs and ruining potential marketing deals, get your lawyers involved and sue the tabloids like the Beckhams. It's imperative to get your good brand name back.

•DID YOU KNOW?•

Comedian David Spade reportedly handed out his sister-in-law's purses to other celebrities to help start up her business. Kate Spade's, *www. katespade.com*, name will forever be linked with expensive fashionable handbags, thanks in part to David. And the Olsen twins (oops, we mean the Olsen sisters), Mary-Kate and Ashley, are reportedly worth $150 million each! Their company Dualstar Entertainment made one billion dollars last year!

Baby Boom

Another way to keep your celebrity brand name from disappearing and keep your fame going is to get pregnant, especially if you're very young (like Kate Hudson, or in your forties, like Geena Davis, Marcia Gay Harden and Helen Hunt) and the baby's father is also a celebrity. Keep in mind -- a well-timed pregnancy can get your name back in the news and keep you from becoming a celebrity-in-crisis. Speculations on a Jennifer Lopez pregnancy has switched the media's focus away from her breakup with Ben Affleck and third marriage to Marc Anthony. No one remembers Gwyneth Paltrow's recent questionable movie choices like "Shallow Hal," "Bounce," and "Duets." All anyone's talking about is her baby daughter's name Apple. Sarah Jessica Parker's HBO series "Sex and the City" was ending, but Parker's fame keeps going with the birth of son James. Watching Paltrow's, Parker's, and Hudson's stomachs expand became a yearlong media event. The paparazzi watched Julia Roberts as she made room for twins. And of course, all eyes are on Jennifer Aniston's and Britney Spears' midriffs. This Hollywood baby boom trend is not going away any time soon.

Your baby gifts, such as a charmeuse silk baby throw, fancy prams, and diaper bags, antique baby cribs, and silver rattles will certainly wind up in the magazines along with your name and photo. Brooke Shields had been out of the spotlight for a while, but now she's writing a book on postpartum depression, *Down Came the Rain: My Journey Through Postpartum Depression*, and is a baby formula spokesmom, *www.brightbeginnings.com*. Having a baby adds more marketing possibilities. Let's face it -- you can't afford not to.

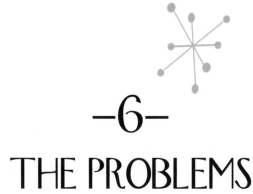

–6–

THE PROBLEMS

"Being famous was extremely disappointing for me. When I became famous it was a complete drag, it is still a complete drag."

Van Morrison -- Irish Musician

One of the problems with being a celebrity is never being allowed to have problems. The media was all over Mariah Carey when she collapsed from exhaustion at her mother's house. Sadly, too much pressure is a downside for many celebrities and it's hard to handle. Sarah Jessica Parker said in *W* magazine (which of course featured her perfect figure just after giving birth) that the standard for celebrities to look gorgeous is too high. But don't worry. We're here to help. Sometimes you really do need a break from cultivating your fame.

We suggest the private Golden Door spa in California, *www. goldendoor.com*. The paparazzi will not be able to find you here, and more importantly, neither will your manager. The Skin Spa is the European day spa for instant relaxation, *www.skinspa.com*, and Canyon Ranch, *www.canyonranch.com*, will make you forget your problems in no time. The Stone Spa, *www.stonespa.com*, the expert on hot stone therapy, has some pretty hot celebrity clientele, including Gwyneth Paltrow, Christy Turlington and Donna Karan.

Defending Yourself

Unfortunately, another downside to fame is the risk of being stalked or kidnapped. Former Spice Girl Victoria Beckham was shocked when nine people were arrested for plotting to kidnap her as she left her home. FBI agents donned tuxedos and walked Russell Crowe down the red carpet at the Golden Globes because they had been tipped off that an attempt was underway to capture the award-winning Gladiator. Brad Pitt and Jennifer Aniston had to call the police to escort them out of a furniture store because so many fans mobbed them as they were shopping one afternoon. David Letterman, Madonna, and Catherine Zeta-Jones have all had problems with stalkers. Actress Rebecca Schaeffer from the sitcom "My Sister Sam" was killed in 1989 by a deranged celebrity fan. This is serious stuff. As your popularity soars it may be necessary to bring a security detail along with you.

Protection, protection, and protection -- we can't stress that enough. You must "release the hounds." Get some dogs to guard your dogs. Howard Rodriguez started the California K9 Academy, *www.californiak9.com*, and his German shepherds have protected Britney Spears' doghouse. And when traveling overseas, make sure your assistant gets you a bodyguard from Blackwater Security Consulting, *www.blackwatersecurity.com*. These guys are former special operation commandos and they're tough.

•*DID YOU KNOW?*•

Actor Michael Clarke Duncan was a bodyguard who watched over Will Smith and Martin Lawrence before he broke into the business. Anyone messing with him might have to walk the "Green Mile." And Marc Anthony reportedly has a license to carry a .45 pistol. You never know -- he might just have it on him for protection.

•MUST DO•

Treat your bodyguard as a bodyguard, not your personal assistant. Your bodyguard is there to save your life, not to hold your purse. Scott Helvenston, fitness instructor, trainer, and stunt man who helped Demi Moore get ready for her role as a Navy Seal in "G.I. Jane," was among four Americans killed in Fallujah, Iraq in an ambush. He was working for Blackwater Security Consulting. Needless to say, protection is a serious and dangerous business. Your guard dogs are also there for protecting, not accessorizing.

Dating Dilemmas

Celebrity dating, of course, is never easy, especially if you are trying to keep it private. The best way to get around this is to only plan on having lunches. Lunches can be dates disguised as "business" meetings. No one needs to know that it's personal business. Mathew Perry and Selma Blair were seen together having lunch and grabbing coffee, but were never linked romantically. This is precisely how you want it to be!

•DID YOU KNOW?•

In general, state laws prohibit news organization from insinuating that you're romantically involved with another celebrity if you happen to be spotted together. For example, you can sue a newspaper if it prints a photograph of the two of you having lunch and implies that you're dating. Keep this in the back of your mind and ask your lawyer to look into this.

You'll need to seek out a mate without seeking out the paparazzi. Jill, Amber and Christie Kelleher run Kelleher & Associates, an exclusive dating service with offices across the country, *www.kelleher-associates.com*.

If you wind up with a celebrity mate, be careful. Even if you're engaged, you never know how long that relationship's going to last. You don't want your career to be overly associated with your celebrity mate. Ben and Jennifer became one celebrity entity nicknamed "Bennifer," which in hindsight was not exactly the greatest career move on their part. Their break-up was such big news it was even reported by The Associated Press, which is one of the problems with making your personal life public. Actor Ralph Fiennes told CBS' "The Early Show," "People make choices whether they want to make their private life public or not. I live with a great actress, Francesca Annis, and we go out. When we go out, we don't, as it were, campaign to get media attention. I don't think that's what we feel like doing." We think that's pretty good advice. So if you and your celebrity partner are not prepared to walk down the red carpet together for the rest of your lives, don't. And if there are high odds on the boards in Vegas against your celebrity marriage lasting, this is not a good way to start out. It means your love life has definitely been overexposed, and it's time to get it out of the limelight and gossip columns.

> **IN**
> Bringing your mom with you to walk down the red carpet or to receive your award.
>
> **OUT**
> Bringing your celebrity squeeze of the moment-- you don't want your temporary relationship to get more attention than you.

•MUST DON'T•

Coping with the paparazzi as you lose your privacy is never easy, but don't get physically violent or you might be arrested for aggravated assault. According to New Jersey law, "A person is guilty of assault if he attempts to cause or purposely, knowingly or recklessly causes bodily injury to another," *www. judiciary.state.nj.us*. So watch that celebrity temper. No punching, kicking, biting or camera smashing. And if the police are called to the scene, it becomes a matter of public record, which means that anyone and everyone will read about your mishap. To help keep this in mind, check out *www.thesmokinggun. com/mugshots*. These photos just might scare you straight and you'll think twice before striking first. Remember, just because you're a celebrity doesn't mean you own the sidewalks. They are public domain and the First Amendment protects the photogs.

Tips to Keep The Paparazzi Away
•Arm your people with flashlights and shine them at the photographers. They can't capture your image if they're blinded by white light.
•Have your security hold big signs in front of you to block

the photogs.

•Keep your nose clean, literally. If you don't want to be taken in a bad light, don't put yourself there. Walking the red carpet and a perp walk is just not the same thing. Doing illegal drugs, carrying concealed weapons, and committing sexual assault – bad career moves. The press will be all over you.

•Don't travel in a pack. Large numbers of your entourage swarming around you only draws attention.

•Last but not least, stay home! Courteney Cox Arquette has been known to throw karaoke parties at home so there aren't any public recordings or videotapes that could be potentially embarrassing!

Of course, if you're Salman Rushdie, you've had more than the paparazzi after you --you've had a fatwa on your head. Making millions of Muslims angry is a major celebrity problem. He had to go into hiding after the 1989 release of his book, *The Satanic Verses*. But since his death sentence has been lifted he's back to living a relatively normal celebrity life, like running from the paparazzi with his former young actress girlfriend, Sophie Dahl or his new bride, Padma Lakshmi.

Meltdowns

If you didn't get the trailer or tour bus you wanted, a severe tantrum or meltdown might be in order. Remember, a semi-annual nervous breakdown goes with the spotlight territory. But the breakdown has to be timed just right -- when you need the publicity, like just after your embarrassing sex tape has come out. It has to appear that you've been working yourself too hard, running yourself ragged, and that no super human being, not even a celebrity, could handle that amount of stress or scrutiny. And you didn't realize you were being filmed in your hotel room or on your boat.

Where you go for rehabilitation after your breakdown is key. The homey Silver Hill in Connecticut has reportedly been the rehab center of choice for celebrities such as Nick Nolte, Billy Joel, and Liza Minnelli. Ben Affleck, Paula Poundstone, and Kelly Osbourne reportedly rehabbed at Promises, the Malibu facility. Cindy McCain, wife of Arizona senator and former Presidential candidate John McCain, joined Narcotics Anonymous after becoming addicted to painkillers. Mary-Kate Olsen checked into the Cirque Lodge for her eating disorder problems.

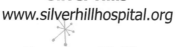

•*DID YOU KNOW?*•

Eric Clapton founded Crossroads Centre Antigua, *http://crossroadsantigua.org*, to help people and families with alcohol and drug abuse and other addictive behaviors.

Rehab

Silver Hills
www.silverhillhospital.org

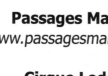

Promises Malibu
www.promises.com

Narcotics Anonymous
www.na.org

Passages Malibu
www.passagesmalibu.com

Cirque Lodge
www.cirquelodge.com

Cedars-Sinai Addiction Medicine Services
www.csmc.edu

www.drug-rehabilitation.org is a comprehensive website to find rehab treatment by state, and to learn what to look for in a rehab center. Have your assistant research this for you.

•DID YOU KNOW?•

Good news for celebrities and their privacy! Supermodel Naomi Campbell won a landmark court case against the British tabloid *Daily Mirror*. The court ruled the tabloid invaded her privacy by reporting, albeit correctly, that the model had visited Narcotics Anonymous. The tabloid was ordered to pay Campbell $6,300 and her legal fees.

Top 10 Celebrity Sex Scandals

Paris Hilton and Rick Salomon video • 2003

Pamela Anderson and Tommy Lee video • 1997

Rob Lowe video • 1988

Michael Jackson's sexual molestation allegations • 1993

Michael Jackson's sexual molestation allegations, Part Deux • 2003

Tonya Harding's wedding video • 1994

Pamela Anderson and Poison's Bret Michaels video • 1998

Frank Gifford and alleged paramour Suzen Johnson in a New York hotel room • 1997

Dr. J. Julius Erving and alleged lady friend video • 2004

Vince Neil's sex video with two centerfold models • 1998

Celebrity Justice

Remember, nothing's more attractive to the paparazzi than a good celebrity gone bad, particularly with the law. Athletes are especially vulnerable in this area. We can't stress this enough: if you don't want negative paparazzi attention, don't give them a reason to take or draw your picture in court.

•DID YOU KNOW?•

When you're famous and your family has problems, their problems become fuel for the tabloid fodder. Reese Witherspoon's brother has been in trouble with the law. If her name wasn't in the papers, probably neither would her brother John's.

Money-Aches

Bad business investments are also serious celebrity problems. People will want to take advantage of your fame and make a buck or two for themselves. Beware of money scams. Former money-manager Dana Giacchetto of the Cassandra Group had celebrity clients like Cameron Diaz and Ben Stiller. Giacchetto was charged with allegedly siphoning off some of his not-so-famous clients' funds and diverting them to his celebrity clients' accounts. Don't let this happen to you. Maybe Wayne Rogers, the former "M.A.S.H." actor, can take a look at your finances. Rogers gives investment advice on the Fox News Channel and has advised celebrities like James Caan and Peter Falk. He is co-chairman of Stop-N-Save, a convenience store chain, and co-chairman of the bridal retailer Kleinfeld.

People will drop your name to help boost their fame. If

you're a megastar this is inevitable. People will try to capitalize on your fame. Pick your battles, and have your lawyer's numbers handy at all times.

One of the most important financial arrangements is your pre-nup. Before you tie the knot, make sure you sign on the dotted line before your spouse's extravagant $300,000 monthly expenses wind up on The Smoking Gun, *www. thesmokinggun.com.*

•MUST DO•
Get a pre-nup.

•MUST DON'T•
Whatever you do, do not give power of attorney to your accountant. BIG MISTAKE!

−7−

THE PERKS

"The nice thing about being a celebrity is that when you bore people, they think it's their fault."
Henry Kissinger -- Former Secretary of State

You're a bona fide celebrity if you're getting free stuff. This can range from a ride to the airport, a Rolex watch, and Armani outfits for the next benefit or even lap dances at Scores. You need to graciously accept the outfit and unwittingly get a matching necklace out of the deal. Learn to sniff out all the free goodies that await you.

Designers/Friends

Lara Flynn Boyle once said that it was hard to look classy before becoming a celebrity because you had to buy your own clothes. But once you become a celebrity people are begging you to wear their frocks. Liz Hurley is quoted as saying about the famous Versace dress held together by safety pins, "That dress was a favor from Versace because I couldn't afford to buy one. His people told me that they didn't have eveningwear, but there was one item left in their press office. So I tried it on and that was it."

So find a designer that you like and become their friend. Gwyneth Paltrow can be seen partying away in Tom Ford and then donning Gucci duds on the red carpet. Elizabeth Hurley lists Donatella Versace as one of her best friends, as well as outfitters. Salma Hayek is reportedly friends with Narciso Rodriguez and has been known to drop by his offices for a visit. Barbra Streisand and Donna Karan are friends.When you rank high enough to call a designer your "friend" then you'll have no problem "borrowing" from them.

The Good Stuff

When it comes to free stuff -- gift bags are the ticket. The value of the gifts inside goodie bags has skyrocketed. Take what you can get; they will make wonderful birthday presents. The most notorious and sought after bag is the Oscar goodie bag. In recent years these bags have contained everything from Lasik eye surgery, to a four-night stay in Switzerland. Keep in mind that the designers, cell phone companies, doctors and hotels want you to use their products because your image boosts their image.

•DID YOU KNOW?•

The 20 actors and actresses nominated at the 2004 Academy Awards received luxury goodie bags worth more than $12,000. Included in the bags was an Eddie Bauer Seattle Suede Jean Jacket, *www.eddiebauer.com*, valued at almost $200. Some of 2005 nominees received beaded handbags and enriched-pearl extract hair syrum. This loot alone is worth $2,000. Typically, goodie bags filled with free trips, exotic car rentals, and jewelry can be worth more than $20,000.

Hotels, cruise lines, corporations and designers line up to give celebs freebies and even money. Celebs can get thousands of dollars from the Paris and New York fashion shows just to be seen sitting in the front row.

In addition to the free stuff, you'll never have to pay for another meal again. When you dine with your agent, he pays. It's a business expense for him. To be on the safe side, never carry money with you. This way, others will have to pay, and you'll just look like an eccentric creative person. And restaurants want you to be seen eating at their establishments, so often it's on the house.

If invited to fund-raising sporting events for various charities, like a golf or tennis tournament -- go! You'll be put up in $3,500 a night suites in five-star hotels with all expenses, such as spa treatments, and meals... paid.

Don't shy away from being a host like Lindsay Lohan at award shows like the MTV Movie Awards. This is a great way to keep your fame going and you might just be treated to freebie shopping and get to choose among leather goods, jewelry, designer shoes and beauty products, in addition to the already pricey goodie bags from the shows.

•DID YOU KNOW?•

Backstage Creations, *www.backstagecreations.com,* puts together awards show packages and celebrity freebies. They've mastered the art of celebrity gift-giving. Celebrity presenters and performers are provided exclusive access backstage at television award shows in a room called "The Retreat" where they get to choose the gifts they want. On their website you can find the list of awards shows for which they've come up with the goods, such as the People's Choice Awards, MTV Music Video Awards, and the NAACP Image Awards.

Some of "The Retreat" Treats

Adidas
Aramis grooming products
AOL lifetime membership
Baccarat jewelry
Canon
Coach watches
Tommy Hilfiger
Kodak
Nike
Ole Henrickson face/body products
Palm handhelds
Red Envelope Spa in a Box
The Sports Club/LA
Sprint PCS
TiVo with lifetime service

Buzz Bags, *www.buzzbags.com*, is also in on the goodie-bag act. Companies place their products in the Buzz Bags given out at celebrity, sports and charity events, film wrap parties, Broadway premieres and more.

Some Buzz Bag Goodies

Kenneth Cole	Lee Jeans
Crunch Fitness	Prescriptives
Frederic Fekkai	Rembrandt Toothpaste
Godiva	Victoria's Secret
Givenchy	Shisheido
Hyatt Regency	Sundance Channel
Ralph Lauren	Tumi

·MUST GO·

Important Awards Shows

Academy Awards
www.oscar.com
Grammy Awards
www.grammy.com
Emmy Awards and Daytime Emmy Awards
www.emmys.com
TONY Awards
www.tonys.org
People's Choice Awards
www.cbs.com
Golden Globe Awards
www.thegoldenglobes.com
Screen Actors Guild Awards
www.sagawards.org
Independent Spirit Awards
www.ifp.org
MTV Video Music Awards and MTV Movie Awards
www.mtv.com
American Music Awards
www.abc.go.com/primetime/ama/
TRL Awards
www.mtv.com
Teen Choice Awards
www.teenpeople.com
Nickelodeon Kids' Choice Awards
www.nick.com
TV Land Awards
www.tvland.com/awards/
Academy of Country Music Awards
www.acmcountry.com

BET Awards
www.bet.com
Billboard Music Awards
www.billboard.com
ASCAP Pop Music Awards
www.ascap.com
Council of Fashion Designers of America (CFDA) Awards
www.cfda.com
Native American Music Awards
www.nammys.com

•MUST DO•

You're going to be invited to party after party, award show after award show. This is not just fun -- this is a competitive sport. You have to out shine everyone at the event, especially at the Oscars and Grammys, even if this means preparing for it all day. When in Hollywood, the more tanned perfect skin showing, the better.

Jim Caviezel played Jesus in a Mel Gibson movie, and got to meet the Pope. If you're a serious Catholic this is a major perk of being a celebrity. If you're an anglophile like Madonna, you might just meet the Queen.

In addition to the free stuff, free meals, and meetings with the Pope, your fans will constantly boost your ego with free love and adoration, supplying your emotional needs with unconditional idol worshipping. This is the plus side to being a celebrity. If you ever feel down because Russell Crowe dumped you and then got married, take a turn down the red carpet and get your dose of love. It will do wonders for your ego and is the easiest way to get that Sally Field "you like me, you really like me!" feeling.

•MUST HAVE•

If you spend about $5000 a month, or $150,000 a year, you might just be invited to receive the exclusive American Express Centurion Card, *http://home.americanexpress.com*. With this card, you can shut down an entire mall for your shopping rampage. This exclusive and respected card will get you the best seats in the house, first class upgrades, a personal travel agent, expert concierge service, after-hours shopping at stores like Valentino, and unlimited credit. You can buy your Porsche on the spot with this baby. This renowned piece of black plastic is not just a credit card, it's a celebrity status card. The annual fee -- approximately $2,500.

When you're a celebrity the perks are never-ending. You can get the movie studios to fly you on private jets, arrange for limousines at your beck and call, and pay for your personal chefs, nannies, makeup artists, hairdressers, assistants, and any other members of your team. Private guards can watch your car, paint your hotel rooms to the color of your liking, and make sure there's champagne and roses in the room. The studios can get you special exercise trailers. As you can see, despite some of the problems, it's not so bad being a celebrity.

–8–

HOW TO RELAX

"A star on a movie set is like a time bomb. That bomb has got to be defused so people can approach it without fear."
Jack Nicholson -- American Actor

Your vacation spot is just as important as your next project. You never want to be out of the spotlight for too long, even if you need to recharge (this is only if you're not on the verge of a breakdown). From places such as Colorado, Florida, the Caribbean, and Europe, you need to know where to stay, what to expect and, as always, where to be seen. Nothing is cuter than a celebrity looking great in a ski outfit or bikini. Just make sure you keep that top on or else you could have another miserable lawsuit on your hands. Mariah Carey was spotted vacationing in chilly Aspen, wearing a low-cut blouse with a warm parka over it, but of course the parka was wide open. That's the way to do it!

Colorado

With Rodeo Drive-esque boutiques, Aspen is a home away from home to the likes of Jack Nicholson, Kevin Costner, Goldie Hawn, Robert McNamara and Michael Eisner.
Melanie Griffith and Antonio Banderas have a cabin behind the Aspen Mountains. John Oates from Hall and Oates has a turkey farm in Woody Creek. And how could we forget– Aspen is where Ivana and Marla fought over "The Donald."

Don Johnson dines at The Caribou Club, *www.caribouclub. com*. Tennis great Martina Navratilova plays at the Aspen Club and Spa, *www.aspenclub.com*. Mariah Carey parties at La Plage and has been seen at Aspen's St. Regis. Princess Diana enjoyed skiing at Beaver Creek, in Vail. Former President Gerald Ford and Oscar winner Tom Hanks have homes there. Mary-Louise Parker, Billy Crudup and Kelsey Grammer have relaxed at the Ritz-Carlton Bachelor Gulch in Avon, Colorado.

Florida

Actor Tommy Lee Jones decided to build a state-of-the-art polo club on his 40-acre horse farm in Wellington, Florida, in Palm Beach County, the U.S. equestrian capital. Rod Stewart has a villa in Palm Beach not far from Donald Trump's members-only Mar-a-Lago Club, *www.trumpnational.com*. Friends Regis and Joy Philbin are frequent visitors. P. Diddy and Pink have reportedly been known to party into the wee hours of the morning in South Beach. And tennis star Venus Williams has relaxed at the Anushka Spa and Sanctuary at the Palm Beach Gardens, *www.aai.com*.

Places to stay in Palm Beach
Everglades Club • 356 Worth Avenue, Palm Beach, FL 33480

Brazilian Court Hotel • 301 Australian Avenue, Palm Beach, FL 33480
Colony Hotel • *www.thecolonypalmbeach.com*, 155 Hammon Avenue, Palm Beach, FL 33480
The Breakers • *www.thebreakers.com*, One South County Road, Palm Beach, FL 33480

When in Palm Beach, make sure you belong to the Palm Beach Polo & Country Club, *www.palmbeachpolo.com* for golf, tennis, and of course, polo.

Madonna and family have stayed at the Raleigh Hotel in Miami, *www.raleighhotel.com*. Britney worked on her tan at the Four Seasons, *www.fourseasons.com/miami*.

The Hamptons
Billy Joel, Christie Brinkley, and the Spielbergs have homes in the Hamptons. Dan Rattiner, publisher of the local *Dan's Papers*, wrote *Who's Here: The Heart of the Hamptons*. It's a who's who of celebrities in the heart of the Hamptons.

Other Hamptonites
Alec Baldwin
Ellen Barkin
Claudia Cohen
Richard Gere
Donna Karan
Calvin Klein

Ron Perelman
Jerry Seinfeld
Renée Zellweger
Sarah Jessica Parker
Ralph Lauren
Matt Lauer

On the East Coast, Nantucket and Martha's Vineyard are vacation and relaxation spots for Carly Simon, James Taylor, Walter Cronkite, the Clintons, writers Art Buchwald and William Styron, Ted Danson, Mike Nichols, Diane Sawyer and John Kerry and wife Teresa.

Debra Winger, Anjelica Houston, Barbra Streisand, Steven Segal, Steven Spielberg and his actress wife, Kate Capshaw, have been known to get away to the Fairmont Miramar Hotel in Santa Monica, *www.fairmont.com*. The relaxation sanctuary Two Bunch Palms Resort & Spa in Desert Hot Springs, California, *www.twobunchpalms.com*, is another celebrity favorite.

Caribbean

The crystal blue waters of the Caribbean attract celebs like Brad Pitt and Jennifer Aniston, Demi Moore and Sharon Stone. Director Steven Spielberg, David Letterman, Beyoncé Knowles, Jay-Z, Kate Moss, Uma Thurman and Billy Joel have vacationed in St. Barts. Billy Crystal and Robin Williams have vacationed in the Bahamas.

•DID YOU KNOW?•

Necker Island, *www.virgin.com/subsites/necker/*, in the British Virgin Islands is a private island owned by Virgin tycoon Sir Richard Branson. It can only accommodate 26 people at a time. Mel Gibson is a reported visitor.

Other Hot Spots

Hawaii is another Hollywood vacation hot spot. Sarah Michelle Gellar and Freddie Prinze, Jr. took a romantic getaway to Maui, where they stayed at the Four Seasons Resort, *www.fourseasons.com/maui/index.html*. Ben Stiller, Helen Hunt, and Dustin Hoffman have also been known to hang-ten in Maui.

Anna Kournikova and Enrique Iglesias were spotted frolicking on the beaches of Bali, Indonesia. Nicole Kidman, Pierce

Brosnan, and Michelle Pfeiffer are reportedly fans of the Wakaya Club in Fiji, *www.wakaya.com.*

Across The Pond

If you want to practice your Italian, you can join Catherine Zeta-Jones and Michael Douglas in Florence (or at Ariel Sands in Bermuda), and Sting and his family in Tuscany. Or catch up with Mel Gibson in Rome, George Clooney in the village of Laglio near Lake Como, and Jon Bon Jovi and Denzel Washington on the Italian island of Sardinia. Jack Nicholson and Naomi Campbell have vacationed on the French Riviera at St. Tropez.

Feeling romantic? Honeymoon in style and go to the San Ysidro Ranch, *www.sanysidroranch.com,* in the foothills of Santa Barbara, or Las Ventanas *www.lasventanas.com,* in Los Cabos, Mexico. Gwyneth Paltrow and Chris Martin spent their first days as husband and wife there. Kate Beckinsale and new husband, director Len Wiseman, honeymooned in Cabo San Lucas, Mexico. Tori Spelling and husband Charlie Shanian honeymooned in Venice and Italy's Lake Como. "The Bachelorette's" Trista and Ryan went to Fiji's Turtle Island, *www.turtlefiji.com.* The Federline's honeymooned in Fiji as well. Singer Thalia and Sony's Tommy Motttola celebrated their union in the Greek Islands. Newlyweds Barbra Streisand and James Brolin honeymooned in Barbados. Check out Elizabeth Arrighi Borsting's *Open Road's Celebrity Weddings and Honeymoon Getaways* if you're interested in more honeymoon destinations.

•*DID YOU KNOW?*•

More and more young stars are tying the knot sooner rather than later. Kate Hudson was 21 when she married Chris Robinson, 34. Jessica Simpson was 22, Brandy was also 22, country singer LeAnn

Rimes was 19, and Beyoncé Knowles' younger sister, Solange, was 17. Kelly Rowland of Destiny's Child and Dallas Cowboy Roy Williams are on the way to the altar. They're both 23.

Concierges-Extraordinaire

If you can't find the time to plan the celebrity vacation of your dreams, Bill Fischer is the New York City travel agent with A-list clients like Tom Cruise, Oprah and Tiger Woods. This midtown Manhattan lifestyle manager-extraordinaire of Fischer Travel Enterprises reportedly requires two recommendations, a $10,000 fee to join, and a yearly $5,000 retainer.

Quintessentially, the United Kingdom based, global, members-only concierge service, *www.quintessentially.com*, offers thousands of benefits, from travel advice, to exclusive club and spa access and the best tables in the finest restaurants. This company reportedly made arrangements for Kate Moss and Gwyneth Paltrow. The membership costs approximately $1,000 per person/per year. Having other people take care of your travel arrangements is definitely relaxing.

Time and Place, *www.timeandplacehome.com*, provides luxury short-term lodging for the distinguished traveler throughout the U.S., Europe, and the Caribbean. This company can even staff your vacation estate with all the luxuries you require. You can feel the tension melting away already.

•DID YOU KNOW?•

InStyle magazine, *www.instyle.com*, has a "Travel Like a Star" section so you can track where the celebs have been and see how they traveled in style.

Inner Peace

You must find the right celebrity religion in order to find some inner peace, while projecting a trendy spiritual image. Whether you become a Buddhist, Scientologist or a plain old Catholic, your religious beliefs will create a buzz and are one of the tools you will use to remain in the spotlight. Lisa Marie Presley said she found comfort and acceptance amongst her fellow Scientologists after a painful divorce. Even if you don't use your religion as part of your marketing scheme, you'll be asked about it and therefore you must be prepared to answer. There are numerous religious opportunities.

•*DID YOU KNOW?*•

Uma Thurman's father is a Buddhist scholar, author, and former monk, *http://literati.net/Thurman*.

Celebrity Scientologists

Kirstie Alley
Tom Cruise
Jenna Elfman
Lisa Marie Presley
Kelly Preston (Mrs. Travolta)
John Travolta

•MUST DO•

To be in the know, find out about the Beverly Hills Kabbalah Centre, *www.kabbalah.com*. If you're not in California, don't worry -- there are 50 other Kabbalah Centre locations, including London. You can check out the online courses, books and audio/ video courses, and of course, Kabbalah bracelets (to bring good luck, absorb negative energy and protect against the evil eye) if you can't make it to the center or you want to keep your Kabbalah in the closet. Madonna, Roseanne Barr, Courtney Love, Missy

Elliot, Britney Spears, Paris Hilton, Ashton Kutcher and Demi Moore, and other celebrities are rumored to have expressed an interest in Kabbalah and the center. Its dean and director is Rav Berg, Kabbalist to the stars. You must know who he is, and if you're a real celebrity he might know who you are too.

Kabbalah – The Basics

Kabbalah • means "receiving"

Fulfillment • you have to find it for yourself, nobody else can

The "Light" • metaphor for energy and possibly God

Sharing and giving • ways to reach the "Light" even when, and especially when, it's uncomfortable to do so

Jealous people • not the best idea to share with them or anyone else who may give you the evil eye

•DID YOU KNOW?•

Madonna's daughter, Lourdes, reportedly goes to Spirituality for Kids, *www.spiritualityforkids.com*, a Kabbalah program for spiritually minded children.

And there's another form of 'enlightenment' sweeping the celeb circles: *Knitting.*

Knitting Books

Celebrity Scarves by Trisha Malcolm and Abra Edelman

Hollywood Knits: Thirty Original Designs by Suss Cousins

IN
Knitting is in. Kristin Davis said, "It's the new yoga" -- a hip and productive way to relax. Knit Café just opened on Melrose Avenue in West Hollywood, *www.knitcafe.com*, and in New York there's Knit New York, *www.knitnewyork.com*. Knit or crochet while waiting in your trailer -- that's apparently what Julia Roberts does. She knits while she's making movies, and so do Cameron Diaz and Sarah Jessica Parker.

OUT
Playing cards are out, especially on "Celebrity Poker Showdown" and "Celebrity Blackjack." Gambling is just not cool and neither is having a poker coach. There should be no PDA (public display of addictions), or you'll look like a celebrity-in-crisis.

–9–

CELEBRITY DO–GOODERS

"Fame is only good for one thing – they will cash your check in a small town."
Truman Capote -- American Author, 1924-1984

Fame is not only just good for cashing checks. As a celebrity you can actually help people. The cause you choose is the biggest commitment you will make in your life. This choice will stay with you longer than any of your marriages. Changing your mind in this department will turn you into a celebrity-in-crisis because you never want to look like a hypocrite. There are two major avenues to take, environment and politics -- politics being the trickier route because you may face more opposition. You need to know how to deal with both categories and provide less threatening alternative causes that will make you look just as smart without alienating the business community. For example, Elizabeth Taylor and Sharon Stone support amfAR, *www.amfar.org*, an organization that raises funds to find a cure for AIDS.

Celebrity causes are yet another way to make you feel good about yourself, because you are actually doing a good deed, while providing some extra advertising for yourself and your brand name. Tiger Woods and Bill and Melinda Gates started foundations in their own names. Montel Williams started the Montel Williams MS Foundation, *www.montelms.org.*You get the idea.

Oprah started her Angel Network, *www.oprah.com*. Rosie O'Donnell started the For All Kids Foundation, *www. forallkids.org*. If you don't have time to oversee a foundation of your own, attach yourself to something you care about and through which you can make a difference. U2's Bono, the charity king, lobbied Congress for $435 million to help relieve debt in Third World countries. Katie Couric undergoes an annual colonoscopy on national television to raise awareness for the National Colorectal Cancer Research Alliance, *www.eifoundation.org*. You can go to the Celebrity Ambassadors section and you can find out which celebs are supporting the Entertainment Industry Foundation's efforts to fight colon cancer. Andre Agassi started his own charter school in Las Vegas, *www.agassifoundation.org*. Christopher Reeve started the -- you guessed it -- the Christopher Reeve Paralysis Foundation, *www.apacure.com*. Lance Armstrong has the Lance Armstrong Foundation, *www.laf.org*. And let's not forget the Britney Spears Foundation and the Britney Spears Camp for the Performing Arts, *www.britneyspears. com*.

•*Did You Know?*•

Prince helped Sheila Escoveda, otherwise known as

Sheila E., record her first solo album, *The Glamorous Life*. But Sheila E. has found a way to help children. Her foundation, *www.lilangelbunny.org*, helps abused and abandoned kids through music therapy.

In general, keep in mind that you can't go wrong with kids or animal causes, AIDS, or the environment. Ivana Trump, Mary Tyler Moore, and Bernadette Peters have hosted "Broadway Barks!" for the FIDONYC organization, which finds permanent homes for New York City shelter animals. Ivana Trump has also been involved with the North Shore Animal League, *http://member.nsalamerica.org/site/PageServer*.

Celebs and Some of Their Causes

Roseanne Barr • The Gay & Lesbian Alliance Against Defamation (GLAAD), *www.glaad.org*

Bono • Amnesty International, *www.amnesty.org*, Greenpeace, *www.greenpeace.org*, War Child, *www.warchild.org*, and Jubilee Plus, *www.jubilee2000uk.org*

David Beckham • National Society for the Prevention of Cruelty to Children, *www.nspcc.org.uk*

George Clooney • United Way of America, *http://national.unitedway.org*

Anderson Cooper • American Heart Association, *www.americanheart.org*

Mike Farrell • Human Rights Watch/California co-chair

Laurence Fishburne • UNICEF, *www.unicefusa.org*

Tom Hanks • GLAAD

Jennie Garth • PETA, *www.peta.com*

Danny Glover • served as the first appointed Goodwill Ambassador for the United Nations Development Programme, *www.undp.org*

Angie Harmon • Peace Games, *www.peacegames.org*

Bianca Jagger • (she's the queen, see below) Human Rights Watch, Coalition for International Justice, Creative Coalition, Amnesty International, People for the American Way, Indigenous Development International, served as goodwill ambassador for the Albert Schweizer Institute and many more...

Reba McEntire • Habitat for Humanity, *www.habitat.org*

Julianne Moore • GLAAD, Pediatric Aids Foundation, *www.pedaids.org*

Kate Moss • National Society for the Prevention of Cruelty to Children

Paul Newman • (if Bianca Jagger's the charity queen, he's the king) *www.newsmansown.com*. He's given over $150 million to thousands of charities.

Edward Norton • BP Solar Neighbors Program, *www.bpsolar.com*

Sarah Jessica Parker • UNICEF, *www.unicefusa.org*, appointed U.S. Fund for UNICEF National Ambassador 1997

Julia Roberts • American Red Cross, *www.redcross.org*, UNICEF, Rett Syndrome, *www.rettsyndrome.org*

Jerry Seinfeld • *www.babybuggy.org*

•*DID YOU KNOW?*•

The American Red Cross, *www.redcross.org*, has a National Celebrity Cabinet. Dakota Fanning, Leeza Gibbons, Cuba Gooding Jr., Heidi Klum, Joan Lunden, Julianna Margulies, Marlee Matlin, Tim McGraw, Nicole Miller, Al Roker, Jane Seymour and Randy Travis are some of the celebrity cabinet members.

Some of Bianca Jagger's Awards

1983 • Honorary Doctorate of Humanities degree by Stone Hill College in Massachusetts

1994 • United Nations Earth Day International Award

1996 • Hispanic Federation of New York City's Humanitarian award

1996 • "1996 Woman of the Year" by Boys Town of Italy

1996 • "Abolitionist of the Year" by the National Coalition to Abolish the Death Penalty

1997 • Green Globe Award by the Rainforest Alliance

1997 • Amnesty International/USA Media Spotlight Award for leadership

1997 • Hall of Fame inductee in Miami Children's Hospital Foundation

1998 • American Civil Liberties Union Award

2000 • Champion of Justice Award

InStyle magazine, *www.instyle.com*, has a "causeceleb" feature, so you can closely follow which stars are linked to which causes.

Reality TV stars founded the Reality Cares Foundation, *www.realitycares.org*. Some of the reality TV star supporters come from shows like "Survivor," "Real World," "The Amazing Race," "Average Joe" and "Who Wants to Marry My Dad?"

Just be sure that you find the right fit for you -- one you can stick with. Dropping a cause has the potential to get very ugly. For example, just imagine how much bad press Katie Couric, "America's Sweetheart," would get if she suddenly decided to sever ties with cancer research. What if Rosie O'Donnell said she was sick of helping kids? This is why it's such a huge commitment.

Do not take this decision, or even your right to free speech, lightly. Natalie Maines of the Dixie Chicks had to clarify and then apologize because of backlash over some anti-Bush remarks she made at a London concert. Protesters used a 33,000-pound tractor to destroy Dixie Chicks CDs and some radio stations boycotted their music. Susan Sarandon and Tim Robbins were reportedly asked to stay away from celebrations at the Baseball Hall of Fame because of their anti-war sentiments.

We told you politics is trickier and messier. An online petition, "Citizens Against Celebrity Pundits," was started to speak out against Hollywood's involvement in politics, *www.ipetitions. com/campaigns/hollywoodceleb*. So if you're going to join Hollywood producer Robert Greenwald's organization, Artists United to Win Without War, be prepared to offend your conservative fan-base, *www.winwithoutwarus.org*.

Top 10 Politically Outspoken Celebrities
Ben Cohen (Ben & Jerry's)
Al Franken
Janeane Garofalo
Richard Gere
Madonna
Michael Moore
Sean Penn

Tim Robbins
Susan Sarandon
Barbra Streisand

•*DID YOU KNOW?*•

Tony Goldwyn and Joe Pantoliano are co-presidents of The Creative Coalition, *www.thecreativecoalition.org*, which was founded by Susan Sarandon, Christopher Reeve, Ron Silver and others. It's considered a leading advocacy association of the arts and entertainment community and educates people on First Amendment rights, arts educations and public funding for arts programs. Every self-respecting, outspoken, politically aware celeb should join this organization.

Norman Lear, the television producer of hit shows like "All In the Family," "Good Times," "One Day at a Time," "Maude," and "The Jeffersons," and movies like "Fried Green Tomatoes," and "The Princess Bride," founded People for the American Way, *www.pfaw.org*. This organization is devoted to defending and promoting civil and equal rights and liberties such as freedom of thought, expression and religion.

Ben Cohen (see Top 10 at left) has whipped up more than just delicious ice cream flavors; he created *www.truemajority. com*, his own politically oriented organization. And if you're interested in buying political paraphernalia, you can check out the T-shirts and other stuff at *www.northernsun.com*.

If you're still unsure which cause to choose, you can check out *www.givespot.com*, to see which celebrities are associated with which causes. Who knows -- you could be the next United Nations Goodwill Ambassador like Angelina Jolie.

IN
Red Kabbalah bracelets

OUT
The Lance Armstrong Live Strong bracelets, *www.laf.org* that only cost a dollar, and plain ribbon pins.**

**If you're going to wear ribbon pins against HIV, breast and ovarian cancer, and heart disease, which is, by the way, a celebrity-given, then your ribbon must be jeweled -- the gaudier the better in this category. It shows you've likely donated big bucks to these worthy causes.

–10–

THE CELEBRITY VARIETIES

"Fame and tranquility can never be bedfellows."
Montaigne -- French Essayist, 1533-1592

We believe that knowing how people became famous, whether they were born into fame, earned it, acquired it by accident or by notoriety, or went after it with gusto, will help you decide which type of celebrity you can become and which ones you should avoid. Knowing the differences will give you an insight into your new celebrity world.

There are five different types of fame that we believe exist today: the born famous, the earned famous, the infamous, the accidental famous, and the "I'll-do-anything-for fame" famous. Most of these categories speak for themselves. Some categories you may never be able to be join because of uncontrollable logistics (your mother wasn't Princess Diana or your father President Kennedy). Nonetheless, don't get discouraged. There's a place for you and we are going to help you find it.

This is part of your overall fame education. Knowing who fits into what category and why and finding out where you want to belong is one of the keys to your upcoming success.

The Born Famous

"A very quiet and tasteful way to be famous is to have a famous relative. Then you can not only be nothing, you can do nothing too."
P.J O'Rourke -- American Humorist and Commentator

If you are one of the Kennedy kids or member of the British Royal family then you were born famous. You live on compounds or in palaces, and have titles, like junior, the third, Prince, and Lord. The media watches your every move. If you're Prince Harry and you smoke a joint or don a swastika, it's on CNN. If you're the President's daughters and you're trying to get a drink while underage, your citation is going to make news.

Madonna's children are constantly followed by the paparazzi. Her daughter, Lourdes, or "Lola" as her mother calls her, posed on the cover of *Vanity Fair* when she was only 16 months old. She's not even 10 and wears Burberry. Elizabeth Hurley's little boy, Damian, seems to prefer baby Dior outfits, and was at the center of a paternity suit brought on by multi-millionaire Steve Bing. This pint-sized star was on the cover of *Vanity Fair* before he was eating solid food.

There's nothing quiet and tasteful about Roger Clinton. He parlayed his famous last name into a short-lived music and acting career. He was even able to put out a few albums, and got numerous film and television cameo appearances. We applaud him for riding on his brother's presidential coat tails and mastering the art of fame cultivation.

The Earned Famous

"The fame you earn has a different taste from the fame that is forced upon you."
Gloria Vanderbilt -- American Author and Designer

Born in the former Soviet Union, Mikhail Baryshnikov was 15 when he started ballet classes and then joined the Kirov Ballet company, where he became a soloist.

Nancy Kerrigan began skating lessons at the age of six and won a silver Olympic medal. Serena and Venus Williams picked up tennis racquets when they were just four years old. They made sports history in 2001 when they became the first sisters in more than 100 years to play each other in a U.S. Open final. You can't deny they earned that. Anna Kournikova may never have won a championship, but she has played the game well enough to earn the hearts of male admirers and many endorsement deals. She even had an Internet virus named after her -- now that's fame.

And then there are the child-actors like Jodie Foster who was nominated for an Academy Award at the age of 14 for "Taxi Driver." Anna Paquin won the coveted trophy for her role in "The Piano" at the age of 11, the second youngest person to ever win an OSCAR. This is the most envied of all celebrity categories, since only a small percentage of the population can claim to be a member of this earned celebrity club. *Harry Potter* author J.K. Rowling, *www.jkrowling.com,* who came from meager beginnings, is one of the world's highest paid writers. Between movie deals and her beloved books, she has made approximately one billion dollars, millions of fans across the globe, and reading "cool" again.

William J. Bratton earned a different kind of fame. He's the Chief of Police for the Los Angeles Police Department. Before his move to Los Angeles, Mayor Rudolph Giuliani made Bratton New York's Police Commissioner in 1994. Along with his many achievements, he's also a lecturer and author and has won countless awards and honors. There's nothing like earning fame for serving and protecting the public.

The Infamous

"Fame usually comes to those who are thinking about something else."
Oliver Wendell Holmes -- American Poet, 1809-1894

If you've made it into this category then you've been very, very preoccupied. In fact, you were so engrossed you didn't realize you were on the notoriety fast track to notoriety. Heidi Fleiss and Monica Lewinsky gained national attention by their naughty deeds. If you become infamous we hope you'll learn from these sexy bad girls. Heidi Fleiss developed a line of clothing and lingerie, Heidi Wear, *www.heidifleiss. com.* Lewinsky turned her infamy into a tell-all book and a line of designer handbags, *www.therealmonica.com.* Gennifer Flowers gained her notoriety when she nearly derailed Bill Clinton's presidential campaign. This year she made her New York supper club singing debut.

Joey Buttafuoco became infamous when his teenaged lover,

Amy Fisher, shot his wife in the head in the early 1990s. In 2003 he was charged with insurance fraud. The "Long Island Lolita" autobiography went on sale in 2005. Prostitute Divine Brown gained notoriety when she was found in Hugh Grant's car. He was arrested for lewd conduct, she appeared on "The Howard Stern Show."

The Accidentally Famous

"Fame is the perfume of heroic deeds."
Socrates -- Greek Philosopher, 470-399 BC

You might just be at the right place at the right time. Chief Charles Moose became the famous mouthpiece and message transmitter to the Washington area serial snipers via the television news. Now he's a celebrity-hero and wrote a book about the experience. Erin Brokovich, the symbol of female chutzpah, helped to win a $333 million lawsuit settlement from Pacific Gas and Electric for the poisoned people of Hinkley, California. An Academy Award winning movie was made about her life story and she now has her own television series on the Lifetime network.

We bet that John Wayne Bobbitt never guessed that he'd become famous for his severed body part. But when fame knocked on his door, he turned his unfortunate accident and miracle of modern medicine into a meal ticket. He bared it all in the porn films "John Wayne Bobbitt Uncut" and "Frankenpenis."

Carolyn Bessette-Kennedy, a former Calvin Klein PR executive, married America's prince and most eligible bachelor. She was nicknamed "Camelot's new queen" and the paparazzi hunt was on, and continues even after her death.

In 2002, Andrew "Jack" Whittaker Jr., from West Virginia won America's largest single lottery payout of more than $300 million after buying more than $100 worth of Powerball tickets- and reportedly managed to get rid of $100 million of it within months of his winning.

The-I'll-Do-Anything-for-Fame -- Anything!

"Fame is proof that the people are gullible."
Ralph Waldo Emerson -- American Poet, 1803-1882

This is our favorite category of all -- the desperately fame-hungry reality TV exhibitionists. These fame seekers are hoping -- no praying -- to cash in on their thirty minutes of fame, and show their "talents," otherwise known as breasts, before the credits roll and the American attention span moves onto something or someone else. If you're a member of this celebrity outcast club you will marry strangers, eat dangerous substances and humiliate yourself just to be on television. Your plan all along was to find the most creative, inventive and preposterous way to get famous. We congratulate you on your shamelessness. Bravo!

However, if you were one of the "star" contestants on "I'm A Celebrity - Get Me Out of Here!" *http://abc.go.com/prime-time/imacelebrity/*, and still think you're a hot celebrity, then you're not only gullible, you are definitely a celebrity-in-crisis.

IN CONCLUSION
ARMED & DANGEROUS

"Be careful what you set your heart upon – for it will surely be yours."
James Baldwin, American Writer 1924-1987

The dictionary defines the word "celebrity" as a famous person of renown. Synonyms for celebrity are: "hero, luminary, name, notable and personage." Don't you see by now how you too can become all these things and much more. Have you noticed yet how your celebrity depends on your sheer determination? Fans will hear your name and rejoice. They will chant your celebrity and seek you out worldwide.

So get off your butt, turn on your computer, log in, and hit this guide hard. Discover your niche and run with it. You don't have to quit your job to do it. There's always time to search the web. And hopefully with our help, you're already better looking and dressed for success, speaking fluent celebrity shtick, and ready for your close-up.

Then, of course, with your fabulous new image you'll be ready to create a buzz. We've shown you how to manufacture your self-invented hype in as many domains as possible. You have to do everything that's legally acceptable to get attention. If you're not famous by now, it's your own darn fault because there are plenty of creative ways to become known.

So it's time to put up, or shut up. But don't say we didn't warn you. You might just get what you wished for!

The Authors

Beth Efran has worked in television production for over 10 years. She started as an assistant for the executive producer of *48Hours*. She became a production associate and a member of the Directors Guild of America. She was promoted to associate director and has directed network television at CBS. During this time, she also worked as a story researcher for the Metro Channel's "Gotham TV" and wrote a syndicated column, "Silicon City," about Internet trends and website reviews. She has also written for *Biography* magazine and others. Beth lives in New York with her husband, a television producer.

Erin Hiner-Gee is a member of the Directors Guild of America and an Associate Director for CBS. Erin started her career in television as an intern at NJN, New Jersey Public Television & Radio. At one time, she worked in public relations for television affiliates across the country. As an associate producer in broadcast marketing, she also led "stakeouts" in Washington D.C. during the Monica Lewinsky/ Bill Clinton scandal. Erin is an accomplished swimmer, married to her college sweetheart and lives in New Jersey.